The Optimist's Handbook

The OPTIMIST'S Handbook

A Companion to HOPE

NIALL EDWORTHY & PETRA CRAMSIE

Free Press

New York London Toronto Sydney

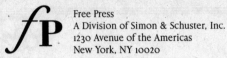

Free Press
A Division of Simon & Schuster, Inc.
1230 Avenue of the Americas
New York, NY 10020

First Free Press trade paperback edition November 2009

FREE PRESS and colophon are trademarks of Simon & Schuster, Inc.

For information about special discounts for bulk purchases, please contact Simon & Schuster Special Sales at 1-866-456-6798 or at business@simonandschuster.com.

The Simon & Schuster Speakers Bureau can bring authors to your live event. For more information or to book an event contact the Simon & Schuster Speakers Bureau at 1-866-248-3049 or visit our website at www.simonspeakers.com.

Designed by Ellen R. Sasahara

Manufactured in the United States of America

10 9 8 7 6 5 4 3 2 1

Library of Congress Cataloging-in-Publication Data

Edworthy, Niall.
    The optimist's handbook : a companion to hope / Niall Edworthy and Petra Cramsie.
        p. cm.
    Title on added title page: Pessimist's handbook : a companion to despair
1. Conduct of life—Humor. 2. Conduct of life—Quotations, maxims, etc. I. Cramsie, Petra. II. Title. III. Title: Pessimist's handbook : a companion to despair.
    PN6231.C6142E39   2008
    082—dc22   041262

ISBN 978-1-4391-0166-7
ISBN 978-1-4391-5953-8 (pbk)

CATEGORIES

ADVENTURE

Only those who dare to fail greatly can ever achieve greatly.
ROBERT F. KENNEDY, 1925–1968, U.S. attorney general

It is not the mountain we conquer but ourselves.
EDMUND HILLARY, 1919–2008, the first man to climb Everest with guide, Sherpa Tenzing

Man cannot discover new oceans unless he has the courage to lose sight of the shore.
ANDRE GIDE, 1869–1951, French writer

We're going to the moon because it's in the nature of the human being to face challenges. It's by the nature of his deep inner soul . . . we're required to do these things just as salmon swim upstream.
NEIL ARMSTRONG, b. 1930, American astronaut

The church says the earth is flat, but I know that it is round, for I have seen the shadow on the moon, and I have more faith in a shadow than in the church.
FERDINAND MAGELLAN, c.1480–1521, Portuguese explorer

Real freedom lies in wildness, not in civilization.
CHARLES LINDBERGH, 1902–1974, American aviator

In 2002, **Brock Enright**, a twenty-five-year-old artist, launched a "designer kidnapping" business for bored New Yorkers looking for some adventure in their lives. Dozens of customers paid Brock and his team between $1,500 and $4,000 to be violently abducted. (Costs varied according to the level of danger involved). Each kidnap was tailored to meet the tastes and phobias of the client, but most chose to be seized, bound, gagged, blindfolded, taken away, and slapped around at a secret location for hours, or even days. Customers were abducted in the street or in their beds at night. "It's about stepping outside of yourself. I wanted to see what I could do," said Jason, a carpenter, after his third abduction.

"It's an incredible bargain at $100 million a seat," says Eric Anderson, president and CEO of Space Adventures, about his plans to fly two private citizens to the far side of the moon. "I believe there's a bigger market than people might imagine." Space Adventures, the pioneers of space tourism, has already flown five customers to the International Space Station (ISS) at a cost to each of roughly $25 million, but the lunar adventure is by far their most ambitious project to date. The U.S. firm promises that for $100 million, the intrepid lunar tourist will get to lead the first important manned space expedition of the twenty-first century, become a catalyst for humankind's expansion into space, join the ranks of the world's greatest explorers, experience the majesty and wonder of earthrise, and explore and experience the far side of the moon.

I am actually not at all a man of science, not an observer, not an experimenter, not a thinker. I am by temperament nothing but a conquistador—an adventurer, if you want it translated—with all the curiosity, daring, and tenacity characteristic of a man of this sort.

SIGMUND FREUD, letter to Wilhelm Fliess dated February 1, 1900

Remember what Bilbo used to say: "It's a dangerous business, Frodo, going out your door. You step onto the road, and if you don't keep your feet, there's no knowing where you might be swept off to."

J.R.R. TOLKIEN, 1892–1973, English novelist

To die will be an awfully big adventure.

J. M. BARRIE, 1860–1937, Scottish novelist and dramatist,
Peter Pan

ADVICE

Live all you can; it's a mistake not to.
HENRY JAMES, 1843–1916, The Ambassadors

Hitch your wagon to a star.
RALPH WALDO EMERSON, 1803–1882, "Society and Solitude"

Whatever you can do, or dream you can, begin it.
Boldness has genius, power and magic in it.
Only engage!
JOHANN WOLFGANG VON GOETHE, 1749–1832

Let us all be happy, and live within our means, even if we have to borrer the money to do it with.
ARTEMUS WARD, 1834–1867, American humorist

Ever tried. Ever failed. No matter. Try again. Fail again. Fail better.
SAMUEL BECKETT, 1906–1989, Worstward Ho

You should make a point of trying every experience once—excepting incest and folkdancing.
Anonymous

Always fornicate between clean sheets and spit on a well-scrubbed floor.
CHRISTOPHER FRY, 1907–2005, The Lady's Not for Burning

It is worth a thousand pounds a year to have the habit of looking on the bright side of things.
SAMUEL JOHNSON, 1709–1784, English writer

My message to you is: Be courageous! Be as brave as your fathers before you. Have faith! Go forward.
THOMAS EDISON, 1847–1931, American inventor

If you are going through hell, *keep going.*
WINSTON CHURCHILL, 1874–1965, British politician

Angels can fly because they take themselves lightly.
G. K. CHESTERTON, 1874–1936, English writer

Alles hat ein Ende, nur die Wurst hat zwei.
Everything has an end, apart from the sausage, which has two.
Austrian proverb

AFTERLIFE

My heaven will be filled with wonderful young men and dukes.

Dame Barbara Cartland, 1901–2000, English romance novelist

Nowadays, carbon-based life-forms don't need to end up as ashes or bones; we can be made into jewelry and be on hand at all times . . . literally. **LifeGem of Chicago** will take a few grains of your cremated remains and subject them to high pressure and temperature. After eighteen weeks, you'll emerge sparkling.

. . . in the next world I shan't be doing music, with all the striving and disappointments. I shall be being it.

Ralph Vaughan Williams, 1872–1958, English composer

How can it enter into the thoughts of man that the soul, which is capable of such immense perfections, and of receiving new improvements to all eternity, shall fall away into nothing almost as soon as it is created?

Joseph Addison, 1672–1719, English essayist

In 1950, when the great enlightened sage **Ramana Maharshi** was on his deathbed, he heard faintly from without the wails and sobbing of those who were preparing to face life without him. A look of bewilderment passed over his face, and he murmured, "But where do they imagine that I could possibly go?"

For the ancient Egyptians, death was a mere break in existence, and nothing to fear if you had a clear conscience. Your friends would mummify you to help you on your way, and you would then, after journeying to the land of the dead, enter the "Hall of Double Justice," in order to affirm to the forty-two judges that you had committed no sin. After having your heart weighed against Truth in a huge pair of scales, Osiris, the God of the Dead, would give judgment. If the scales were in equilibrium he would pronounce in your favor, and from then on you would lead a life of eternal happiness in the kingdom of the dead.

As the self travels in this body from childhood to youth to old age, so the self moves into another body at death. The wise are not confused by this change.
THE BHAGAVAD GITA, 2:12–13

All is not lost! Even wandering spirits can eventually find peace in the Afterlife. **The Chinese** celebrate a Ghost Month, the seventh in the calendar, when the gates of hell are thrust open, liberating hungry ghosts who search the Earth for food or to take revenge on those who have upset them by entering their bodies and causing illness. To entertain these spirits and ward off their evil, people perform street operas, burn "hell money," and cook feasts. The ghosts are then guided with lanterns in the direction of Heaven.

ALCOHOL

Wine is bottled poetry.
ROBERT LOUIS STEVENSON, 1850–1894, Scottish writer

Man, being reasonable, must get drunk;
The best of life is but intoxication.
LORD BYRON, 1788–1824, English poet, Don Juan

Possible health benefits of moderate alcohol consumption:

Lower risk of heart disease and heart attack
Lower risk of stroke
Lower risk of gallstones
Lower risk of diabetes

Beer is proof that God loves us and wants us to be happy.
BENJAMIN FRANKLIN, 1706–1790, American writer, scientist, and diplomat

Our country has deliberately undertaken a great social and economic experiment, noble in motive and far-reaching in purpose.
HERBERT HOOVER, U.S. president on prohibition in 1919

Anthony Burgess's modern classic *A Clockwork Orange* might never have been completed if it wasn't for the numbing effects of booze. "I had to write *A Clockwork Orange* in a state of near drunkenness in order to deal with the material that upset me so much," Burgess recalled.

> No poems can please for long or live that are written by water-drinkers.
>
> *HORACE, 65–8 BC, Roman poet*

A year-long study by Spanish scientists in 2002 involving four thousand volunteers showed that drinking two—but not one or three—glasses of red wine a day halves the chances of catching a common cold.

Well known writers who drank heavily

Samuel Johnson	Evelyn Waugh
John Donne	Ernest Hemingway
Lord Byron	F. Scott Fitzgerald
Oscar Wilde	Dorothy Parker
Eugene O'Neill	Raymond Carver
Kingsley Amis	Truman Capote
Dylan Thomas	Jack London
Malcolm Lowry	William Faulkner
Winston Churchill	Herman Melville

ANIMALS

All the really good ideas I ever had came to me while I was milking a cow.

GRANT WOOD, 1891–1942, American painter

Animals are such agreeable friends—they ask no questions, they pass no criticisms.

GEORGE ELIOT, 1819–1880, Mr. Gilfil's Love Story

ANIMAL RIGHTS PART ONE

Recently, there have been moves toward including certain creatures in a "community of equals" with humans. The Seattle-based **Great Ape Project** is calling for the UN to adopt a **Declaration on Great Apes,** in which chimps, bonobos, gorillas, and orangutans have the right to life, the protection of individual liberty, and the prohibition of torture.

The great pleasure of a dog is that you may make a fool of yourself with him and not only will he not scold you, but he will make a fool of himself too.

SAMUEL BUTLER, 1835–1902, English writer

When the insects take over the world, we hope they will remember with gratitude how we took them along on all our picnics.

BILL VAUGHAN, 1915–1977, American columnist

Chimps are from Mars, Bonobos are from Venus

Whereas the well-known common chimpanzee is marauding, murdering, and brutally dominant, the lesser-known **bonobo** is cooperative, friendly, and peace-loving. So why don't we see more bonobos in zoos? Perhaps part of the answer is that these gentle apes spend an extraordinary amount of time having sex with every member of the group and in every conceivable (and inconceivable) position, which might not suit your average Sunday School outing. In the wild, whereas chimps tend to kill each other during territorial disputes, bonobos usually make love not war, with females rushing to begin an orgy with the enemy which usually ends with all the adults grooming each other while their children play. We share almost 100 percent of our DNA with both kinds of chimp, so is it too much to hope that, one day, we'll allow our inner bonobo out of the bedroom and onto the battlefield?

I find penguins at present the only comfort in life. One feels everything in the world so sympathetically ridiculous, one can't be angry when one looks at a penguin.

JOHN RUSKIN, 1819–1900, English author and poet

ANIMAL RIGHTS PART TWO

The founder of utilitarian philosophy, **Jeremy Bentham,** stated that, when considering whether or not a being should have rights. "The question is not, 'Can they reason?', nor 'Can they talk?' but 'Can they suffer?'" As **People for the Ethical Treatment of Animals** founder **Ingrid Newkirk** says, "When it comes to pain, love, joy, loneliness, and fear, a rat is a pig is a dog is a boy. Each one values his or her life and fights the knife." Throw away your fur coat and go to www.peta.org for more information.

ART & ARTISTS

To be an artist is to believe in life.
HENRY MOORE, *1898–1986, English artist and sculptor*

Art—the one achievement of Man which has made the long trip up from all fours seem well advised.
JAMES THURBER, *1894–1961, from* Forum and Century, *June 1939*

At the age of six I wanted to be a cook. At seven I wanted to be Napoleon. And my ambition has been growing steadily ever since.
SALVADOR DALI, *1904–1989, Spanish surrealist painter*

Cave paintings (usually of wild animals) tell us that Art has been an essential part of the human experience since the dawn of time (or, at least, from 32,000 years ago). We cannot tell what the paintings were "for," whether they were religious, a way of passing on information, or merely ceremonial; perhaps they were simply painted in response to the artistic impulse. To marvel at the beauty of the 16,000-year-old **Lascaux cave paintings** go to: www.culture.gouv.fr/culture/arcnat/lascaux/en

Decorative art does not exist—only art, intimate, heroic or epic.

GEORGE ROUAULT, *1871–1958, from* La Renaissance, *1937*

Art Therapy is a method of using the creative process to improve the mental, physical, and emotional welfare of people. Widely used in hospitals as well as businesses and schools, it is of particular value in helping traumatized children process horrors which they cannot put into words, as workers at **Human Rights Watch** showed when they gave children in Darfur crayons and paper. But children who simply have problems with mainstream school can also benefit. **The Art Room,** a charity based in Oxford, offers art as therapy to many children whose education has been disrupted for one reason or another, with very encouraging results.

The purpose of art is washing the dust of daily life off our souls.

PABLO PICASSO, 1881–1973, Spanish artist

Do not fail, as you go on, to draw something every day, for no matter how little it is it will be well worth while, and it will do you a world of good.

CENNINO CENNINI, c. 1370–c. 1440, Italian painter

There is no must in art because art is free.

WASSILY KANDINSKY, 1866–1944, Russian abstract artist

Don't look for obscure formulas or mystery in my work. It is pure joy that I offer you.

CONSTANTIN BRANCUSI, 1876–1957, Romanian abstract sculptor

Great art picks up where nature ends.

MARC CHAGALL, 1887–1985, Russian painter

BALDNESS

When others kid me about being bald, I simply tell them that the way I figure it, the good Lord only gave men so many hormones, and if others want to waste theirs on growing hair, that's up to them.

JOHN GLENN, b. 1921, American astronaut

The most delightful advantage of being bald—one can *hear* snowflakes.

R. G. DANIELS, *1916–1993, British magistrate*

I don't consider myself bald. I'm simply taller than my hair.

TOM SHARPE, *b. 1928, English author*

Experience is a precious gift, only given a man when his hair is gone.

Turkish proverb

There is more felicity on the far side of baldness than young men can possibly imagine.

LOGAN PEARSALL SMITH, 1865–1946, Afterthoughts (1931)

On first meeting Cecil B. de Mille:

He wore baldness like an expensive hat, as if it were out of the question for him to have hair like other men.

GLORIA SWANSON, 1897–1983, Hollywood star

Sexy, Charismatic, Successful Bald Men

Yul Brynner	Danny de Vito
Telly Savalas	Michael Stipe
Patrick Stewart	Larry David
Sean Connery	Ross Kemp
Vin Diesel	Stone Cold Steve Austin
Bruce Willis	Zinedine Zidane
Jason Alexander	Andre Agassi
Ben Kingsley	Michael Chiklis

There is no consensus as to why male pattern baldness exists, but the most likely theory suggests that it has evolved in males through sexual selection as an enhanced signal of status, social maturity, and ability to maintain a mate in the lifestyle to which she is accustomed. So if you're growing old and shiny-pated, just remember the words of **Dolly Parton**: "I love bald men. Just because you've lost your fuzz don't mean you ain't a peach."

Baldness may well be a blessing, but in October 2006 a UK biotechnology firm announced they could cure it by removing hair follicles from the back of the neck, multiplying them, and then implanting the cells into the scalp. This method of hair multiplication proved successful in 70 percent of male patients, and the treatment will be available to the public by 2009. Another technique has been pioneered in Italy. Pierluigi Santi, of Genoa, has successfully used stem cells to "multiply" hair roots, and his method will soon be available to paying customers.

BEAUTY

"Beautiful! Beautiful!"
Edwin "Buzz" Aldrin, b. 1930, first words as he stepped onto the moon in 1969

If eyes were made for seeing, then Beauty is its own excuse for being.
Ralph Waldo Emerson, 1803–1882

The beauty of creatures is nothing other than the image of the divine beauty in which things participate.
St. Thomas Aquinas, 1225–1274, Commentarium in Dionysii de Divinibus Nominibus, *Book 4, Chapter 5 (1260)*

Knowledge of ideal beauty is not to be acquired. It is born with us.

WILLIAM BLAKE, 1757–1827, annotations to Sir Joshua Reynolds's
Discourses *(1808)*

What the imagination seizes as beauty must be truth—whether it existed before or not.

JOHN KEATS, 1795–1821, letter to Benjamin Bailey, November 22, 1817

There is nothing ugly; I never saw an ugly thing in my life: for let the form of an object be what it may—light, shade, and perspective will always make it beautiful.

JOHN CONSTABLE, 1776–1837, British painter

The beauty of the world is almost the sole way by which we can allow God to penetrate us . . . the beauty of the world is the commonest, easiest and most natural way of approach.

SIMONE WEIL, 1909–1943, Attente de Dieu

It would appear we really are beauty-conscious as human beings! Good looks are worth their weight in gold. Studies from **University of Texas** and **Michigan State University** show that the more attractive you are the more likely you are to earn better money. Basically, unattractive employees earn 5 to 10 percent less than others. Those considered good looking, in turn, earn more than those deemed average in looks.

Researchers at **Columbia University's School of Business** used data from an online dating site (which allows viewers to rate each other's physical appearance) to show that people with comparable attractiveness tend to pair up. Unattractive men, however, are more likely to try to ask unattainable beauties out on a date! To no avail . . .

BOOKS

Books can not be killed by fire. People die, but books never die. No man and no force can abolish memory . . . in this war, we know, books are weapons. And it is a part of your dedication always to make them weapons for man's freedom.

FRANKLIN D. ROOSEVELT, 1882–1945, message to the Booksellers of America, May 6, 1942

The world is a great volume, and man the index of that book.

JOHN DONNE, 1572–1631, sermon from the funeral of Sir William Cockayne, December 12, 1626

People say that life is the thing, but I prefer reading.

LOGAN PEARSALL SMITH, 1865–1946, Afterthoughts, "Myself" (1931)

Studies have shown that American children who learn to read by the third grade are less likely to end up in prison, drop out of school, or take drugs. **Adults who read literature on a regular basis are nearly three times as likely to attend a performing art event, almost four times as likely to visit an art museum, more than two-and-a-half times as likely to do volunteer or charity work, and one-and-a-half times as likely to participate in sporting activities.**

To write the essential book, the only true book, a great writer does not need to invent because the book already exists inside each one of us and merely needs translation.

MARCEL PROUST, *1871–1922, French novelist*, À la recherche du temps perdu *(1927)*

If the dullest person in the world would only put down sincerely what he or she thought about his or her life, about work and love, religion and emotion, it would be a fascinating document.

A. C. BENSON, *1862–1925*, From a College Window *(1906)*

It is not true that we have only one life to live; if we can read, we can live as many more lives and as many kinds of lives as we wish.

Attributed to S. I. HAYAKAWA, *1908–1992*

Men of power have not time to read, yet men who do not read are not fit for power.

MICHAEL FOOT, *b. 1913, British politician and writer*

A book is a version of the world. If you do not like it, ignore it; or offer your own version in return.

SALMAN RUSHDIE, *b. 1947, Indian-British novelist*

BOREDOM

Boredom is the highest mental state.

Attributed to ALBERT EINSTEIN, *1879–1955, German-born physicist*

Don't despair at the sound of that familiar moan from kids, "I'm booooored." According to some child psychologists children need to experience boredom to relax, rest, and initiate social interaction of their own accord. Without a good dose of boredom they'll always seek outside stimulation and spend life with the bitter taste of dissatisfaction in their mouths. In some religious circles, for example within Buddhism and Hinduism, boredom is a path to awakening greater self-awareness. It offers you the chance to empty yourself of superficial needs and feelings. Why not celebrate being bored? Log onto www.bored.com. If even that doesn't make you happily bored, go to www.pointlesssites.com.

What's wrong with being a boring kind of guy?
GEORGE W. BUSH, b. 1946, U.S. president

Extreme boredom serves to distract us from boredom.
FRANÇOIS DUC DE LA ROCHEFOUCAULD, 1613–1680, French writer

Everybody is somebody's bore.
Attributed to EDITH SITWELL, 1887–1964, British poet

It is better that aged diplomats be bored than for young men to die.
WARREN AUSTIN, 1877–1962, a U.S. diplomat on the advantage of lengthy debating at the United Nations

Australian psychologists from Canberra's Australian National University are experiencing close encounters of a new kind—studying boredom in view of *future missions to Mars*. It is feared that astronauts far away from planet Earth for sustained periods may end up so totally bored and lonesome that they may turn on each other with dire consequences for space missions. A simulated Mars base is being constructed in the Australian outback to replicate conditions miles from Earth. People, the world over will be waiting eagerly to hear how to banish boredom from outer space!

CHANGE

The quintessential revolution is that of the spirit, born of an intellectual conviction of the need for change in those mental attitudes and values which shape the course of a nation's development . . . It is not enough to merely call for freedom, democracy, and human rights. There has to be a united determination to persevere in the struggle, to make sacrifices in the name of enduring truths, to resist the corrupting influences of desire, ill-will, ignorance, and fear.

Aung San Suu Kyi, b. 1945, Burmese dissident leader, Nobel Peace Prize speech in 1991

Only idiots don't change.
French proverb

Nothing is so perfectly amusing as a total change of ideas.
Laurence Sterne, 1713–1768, British novelist, Tristram Shandy, *Book 9, dedication*

One of the things I learnt when I was negotiating was that until I changed myself I could not change others.
Nelson Mandela, b. 1918, Sunday Times *of Johannesburg (2000)*

Never doubt that a small band of committed people can change the world. Indeed, it is the only thing that ever has.
Attributed to MARGARET MEAD, *1901–1978*

Alcoholics Anonymous meetings commence with **The Serenity Prayer:**
Lord, grant me the serenity to accept the things I cannot change, the courage to change the things I can, and the wisdom to know the difference.

You must be the change you wish to see in the world.
MAHATMA GANDHI, *1869–1948, Indian political and spiritual leader*

To-day is not yesterday: we ourselves change; how can our Works and Thoughts, if they are always to be the fittest, continue always the same? Change, indeed, is painful; yet ever needful; and if Memory have its force and worth, so also has Hope.
THOMAS CARLYLE, *1795–1881, Essays—Characteristics*

It is change, continuing change, inevitable change, that is the dominant factor of our society . . .
ISAAC ASIMOV, *1920–1992, author, "My Own View" (1978)*

We must obey the great law of change. It is the most powerful law of nature.

A state without the means of some change is without the means of its conservation.
EDMUND BURKE, *1729–1797,* Reflections on the Revolution in France *(1790)*

CIVILIZATION

By the test of our faith the highest standard of civilization is the readiness to sacrifice for others.

DAVID LLOYD GEORGE, 1863–1914, speech in Queen's Hall in 1914

Are we not arrived at the point when there is no longer anything to fear, either from new errors, or the return of old ones; when no corrupt institution can be introduced by hypocrisy, and adopted by ignorance or enthusiasm, when no combination can affect the infelicity of a great people?

MARQUIS DE CONDORCET, 1743–1794, Enlightenment philosopher who believed civilization was heading toward perfection

The first Forum of the **Alliance of Civilizations** took place in Madrid, Spain, in January 2008. The forum brought together international political leaders, government bodies, civil society groups, and philanthropic foundations to examine urgent ways of promoting a mutual understanding of civilizations in the face of growing extremism and polarization of cultures. To symbolize the importance of exchange and dialogue the forum was opened by the prime minister of Spain in partnership with the Turkish prime minister and UN representatives. The Arab League, Queen Noor of Jordan, and Brazilian writer Paulo Coelho were all part of the event.

Civilization (from the Latin meaning city) is nothing more or less than testimony to our superb ability to cooperate. The urban revolution began about five thousand years ago, in several places all over the world, as farming technology—the plough, irrigation, and fertilizers—freed mankind from the overwhelming, day-to-day tyranny of finding food, and men began to build cities, job-share, and specialize: in short, evolve into citizens. The world's first empires, such as that of the Acadians, in Mesopotamia's "Fertile Crescent," and those of Meso-America, were the cradles of astronomy, mathematics, writing, and craftwork; in Africa, people learned to fuse tin and copper to make ornaments and weapons of bronze. Today, cities and all their associated freedoms still appear to be our destiny: in 2008, there were, for the first time in history, more city dwellers worldwide than country dwellers and, by 2030, 5 billion of us will be living urban lives.

Jesus wept and Voltaire smiled. Of that divine teardrop and the sweetness of that human smile present civilisation is made.
Victor Hugo, 1802–1885, speech on Voltaire's centenary, 1878

That's one small step for (a) man. One giant leap for mankind.
Neil Armstrong, b. 1930, American astronaut, spoke these words after landing on the moon July 21, 1969

Doomsters would have you believe that it's all over. However, for the optimistic boomster, human civilization is only just leaving the starting blocks. Scientist **Stephen Hawking** believes that "the long-term survival of the human race is at risk as long as it is confined to a single planet, but once we spread out into space and establish independent colonies our future should be safe."

> Society is indeed a contract . . . it becomes a partnership not only between those who are living, but between those who are living, those who are dead, and those who are to be born.
>
> *EDMUND BURKE, 1729–1797,* Reflections on the Revolution in France *(1790)*

DEATH

What would life be without death—would it be any kind of life at all? The influential **Leon Kass,** a bioethicist at the University of Chicago, is among those who holds that death is what gives our lives shape, for without the definition and certainty it brings, many of the things that give our lives meaning—art, love, beauty—would be lost; while the political economist **Francis Fukuyama** believes that to abandon death would be, essentially, to abandon our humanity; he has called transhumanism "the World's Most Dangerous Idea."

Seven years after death, in a ceremony called the *famadihana*, or turning of the bones, Madagascan people dig their loved ones up and parade their bones around, telling them all the local gossip. The bones are then carefully cleaned and wrapped in a new shroud for reburial. The old shroud is often presented to a newly wed couple in the family for them to make love on, so that the ancestor's power will live on in any children the couple conceives.

Perhaps the best cure for the fear of death is to reflect that life has a beginning as well as an end. There was a time when we were not: this gives us no concern—why then should it trouble us that a time will come when we shall cease to be? . . . To die is only to be as we were before we were born; yet no one feels any remorse, or regret, or repugnance, in contemplating this last idea.

WILLIAM HAZLITT, 1778–1830, "On the Fear of Death"

We can be certain that more than a hundred thousand persons die in the world every day. So that a man who has lived for thirty years has escaped this tremendous destruction about one thousand, four hundred times.

SÉBASTIEN ROCH NICOLAS DE CHAMFORT, 1741–1794

It is impossible that anything so natural, so necessary, and so universal as death, should ever have been designed by Providence as an evil to mankind.

JONATHAN SWIFT, 1667–1745, Thoughts on Religion

An Irish Blessing

May you die in bed at ninety-five,
shot by a jealous spouse.

Eternal law has arranged nothing better than this: that it has given us one way into life, but many ways out.

SENECA, c. 4 BC–AD 65, Roman Stoic philosopher

If you think it would be a shame to die when your turn comes, go to www.alcor.org to find out more about how you, or just your brain, can be preserved after your death. Cryonically suspended in liquid nitrogen at minus 196 degrees, awaiting medical and scientific advances, you may one day be able to take up life again where you left off.

Death belongs to life as birth does. The walk is in the raising of the foot as in the laying of it down.

RABINDRANATH TAGORE, 1861–1941, awarded the Nobel Prize for Literature

I bet you a hundred bucks he ain't in here.

CHARLES BANCROFT DILLINGHAM, 1868–1934, to a fellow pall-bearer at the funeral of escapologist Harry Houdini

DREAMS

We grow great by dreams. All big men are dreamers.
WOODROW T. WILSON, 1856–1924, U.S. president

It is better to dream your life than to live it, and even though you live it, you will still dream it.
MARCEL PROUST, 1871–1922, Les Plaisirs et les Jours (1896)

Come to me in my dreams, and then
By day I shall be well again!
For then the night will more than pay
The hopeless longing of the day.
MATTHEW ARNOLD, 1822–1888, "Longing" (1852)

Since Life is but a Dream, Why toil to no avail?
LI PO, 701–762, Chinese poet

I have a dream. I have a dream that my four little children will one day live in a nation where they will not be judged by the color of their skin but by the content of their character.
MARTIN LUTHER KING JR., 1929–1968, at the March on Washington, June 15, 1963

To dream is happiness; to wait is life.
VICTOR HUGO, Les Feuilles d'automne (1831)

Psychologists estimate that we daydream for about a third to a half of our waking hours. Each single daydream may last only a few seconds or a couple of minutes. Children and adults alike are often chided for daydreaming, yet it fulfills an essential function in our lives. It allows us, for example, to imagine and manage stressful situations and conflict, control our behavior, foresee relationship tensions, relax and recharge our minds, and so on. It can also be a moment of a particular revelation. **Chemist Friedrich August Kekulé, 1829–1896,** puzzled by how the carbon atoms of benzene fitted together, suddenly came to a clear realization while daydreaming on a Clapham omnibus. Next time you see a friend staring into space don't wave your hand in front of his or her eyes.

Dreams pass into the reality of action. From the actions stems the dream again; and this interdependence produces the highest form of living.
Attributed to ANAÏS NIN, 1903–1977, Cuban-French author

A man's dreams are an index to his greatness.
ZADOK RABINOWITZ, 1823–1900, influential Hasidic thinker

Everything you can imagine is real.
PABLO PICASSO, 1881–1973, Spanish artist

DRUGS

I've never had a problem with drugs. I've had problems with the police.

KEITH RICHARDS, b. 1943, member of the Rolling Stones

Thou hast the keys of paradise, oh just, subtle and mighty opium!

THOMAS DE QUINCEY, 1785–1859, Confessions of an English Opium-Eater (1822)

In 1863 Italian chemist **Angelo Mariani** patented a wine called Vin Mariani which contained 12 percent alcohol and 6.5 milligrams of cocaine in every ounce. His Holiness Pope Leo XIII, who carried around a hip flask of the wine, was so impressed he awarded Mariani a coveted "gold medal." Other well-known figures, who innocently enjoyed the effects of cocaine, included the writers **Henrik Ibsen, Émile Zola, Jules Verne, Alexander Dumas,** and **Sir Arthur Conan Doyle. Robert Louis Stevenson** was said to have written *The Strange Case of Dr. Jekyll and Mr. Hyde* during a week-long cocaine binge. Royal dabblers included **Queen Victoria, King Alphonse XIII of Spain,** and **the Shah of Persia,** while U.S. presidents **William McKinley** and **Ulysses S. Grant** were also enthusiasts.

Only when committing adultery.

WYCHE FOWLER, b. 1940, when asked if he smoked marijuana in the 1960s

It's the Real Thing

Concocted by **John Stith Pemberton**, a former lieutenant in the Confederate Army, Coca Cola began life in 1886 as "valuable brain-tonic and cure for all nervous afflictions." The new beverage, sold at chemists across Atlanta, was known as Pemberton's French Wine Coca, and according to the blurb, offered "the virtues of coca without the vices of alcohol." Each recommended serving contained a significant quantity of cocaine until the drug was removed from the production process in 1903.

A radically liberal drug policy introduced in Zurich at the end of the 1990s has led to an 82 percent decline in new users of heroin, according to a report published in *The Lancet* in early 2008. Drug addicts in the Swiss city are offered "substitution" treatment, including injectable heroin, oral methadone, needle exchange, and "shooting galleries" where they can get their fix. The controversial new approach is succeeding, the report says, by removing the perceived glamor of taking heroin and presenting it as a serious illness. "Finally, heroin seems to have become a loser drug, with its attractiveness fading for young people," said Carlos Nordt of the Psychiatric University Hospital in Zurich. While the policy led to a dramatically steep decline in the numbers of new users, the overall number of heroin addicts in the city declined by 4 percent a year.

Drugs may be the road to nowhere, but at least they're the scenic route.
Anonymous

If even a small fraction of the money we now spend on trying to enforce drug prohibition were devoted to treatment and drug rehabilitation, in an atmosphere of compassion not punishment, the reduction in drug usage and in the harm done to users could be dramatic.

MILTON FRIEDMAN, 1912–2006, 1976 Nobel Prize winner for Economics

Popular in the 1930s, the **Brompton Cocktail**, a mixture of cocaine, morphine, alcohol, and sweet syrup was prescribed to terminally ill patients in order to give them a euphoric send-off from this world. So named after the Royal Brompton hospital in London where it was invented, the concoction was also administered as a cough sedative to tuberculosis sufferers.

EDUCATION

Education is a fundamental human right. It is the key to sustainable development and peace and stability within and among countries, and thus an indispensable means for effective participation in the societies and economies of the twenty-first century . . . Achieving Education for All goals should be postponed no longer. The basic learning needs of all can and must be met as a matter of urgency.

UN-sponsored World Education Forum, Dakar, Senegal, April 26–28, 2000

Establishing lasting peace is the work of education; all politics can do is keep us out of war.

Maria Montessori, 1870–1952, Italian educator and humanitarian

Education is the great engine of personal development. It is through education that the daughter of a peasant can become a doctor, that a son of a mineworker can become the head of the mine, that a child of farm workers can become the president of a great nation. It is what we make out of what we have, not what we are given, that separates one person from another.

Nelson Mandela, b. 1918

Each diploma is a lighted match . . . Each one of you is a fuse.

Edward Koch, b. 1924, mayor of New York, addressing students in 1983

Studies coming out of **Harvard Medical School** show that people with more than twelve years of education can look forward to an extra seven years of life compared to those who had twelve or fewer years spent in education. Those who stayed in education the longest can currently expect to live to eighty-two, while those with less time in education only to seventy-five. What was the rush to leave school?

The roots of education are bitter, but its fruit is sweet.

Aristotle, 384–322 BC

Let us reform our schools, and we shall find little need of reform in our prisons.

JOHN RUSKIN, *1819–1900, English author and poet*

Educating girls and women reduces family size, delays marriage, and increases the chances of having and maintaining healthier babies. It is reckoned, by the World Bank and intergovernmental sources, that one year of female education reduces fertility by 10 percent, even more so at secondary level. Women with formal education are more likely to get medical advice, delay marriage, combat HIV/AIDS and disease, and have nutritional knowledge for their children. It also increases women's income and generates greater productivity. A girl who goes to school is also a woman who is more likely to send her own children to school.

Don't wait for schools to be built. Teach the children under the nearest tree.

BIN SAID QABOOS, *b. 1940, Sultan of Oman*

Whoso neglects learning in his youth loses the past and is dead for the future.

EURIPIDES, *480–406 BC*

I have never met a man so ignorant that I couldn't learn something from him.

GALILEO GALILEI, *1564–1642*

ENVIRONMENT

Global Warming: Reasons to Be Cheerful

Longer growing seasons
Less winter transport disruption
Reduced demand for winter heating
Less cold-related illness
Agricultural diversification
Increase in tourism and leisure pursuits
Shift to healthier outdoor-oriented lifestyles

The Kyoto Protocol, in which countries around the world pledged to do their bit in the fight against climate change, is up for renegotiation in 2012. But the United States, which is responsible for a quarter of the world's greenhouse gas emissions, has not participated, believing the protocol gives an unfair advantage to the developing countries. The C&C (Contraction and Convergence) framework conceived by Aubrey Meyer of the Global Commons Institute proposes that the world can decide how much more carbon dioxide it is safe to emit, and can then share that allowance equally—but, crucially, not between *countries*, but *per capita*—carbon rationing, in effect.

We come away from this project with a strong sense that something large, perhaps even revolutionary, is struggling to be born as business leaders, investors, politicians, and the general public create the architecture of sustainable economics. Indeed, it is breathtaking to see how much innovation has been unleashed by the wave of concern about climate change that has broken across the world in the past year, culminating in the awarding of the Nobel Peace Prize to the world's leading climate scientists and their most effective evangelist, Al Gore.

CHRISTOPHER FLAVIN, president of the environmental research organization, Worldwatch Institute

It is easy to be pessimistic in the face of the daunting environmental challenges that every one of us faces. But the prospect of environmental innovation makes me an optimist, at least over the longer term . . . No company or industry can today afford to ignore energy costs, pollution issues, and other environmental challenges. Those that do risk competitive disadvantage.

DANIEL C. ESTY, Hillhouse Professor of Environmental Law & Policy, Yale University, 2008

In 2007, **Richard Branson** launched the Virgin Earth Challenge prize, inviting scientists to invent a method of sucking or "scavenging" one billion tons of carbon dioxide, directly from the sky, per year. He offered $25 million to whoever succeeds in meeting the challenge, but the real prize would be the dramatic impact that this would have on global warming, and thus, as the Virgin boss puts it, "the satisfaction of saving thousands of species and possibly mankind itself."

When, in 2006, a U.S. businessman told the Kenyan environmental activist and Nobel Peace Prize winner **Wangari Maathai** that his company was planning to plant a million trees, she replied, "That's great. But what we really need is to plant one billion trees." So far, she has inspired people to plant a total of 1.5 billion trees, and counting. "The planting of trees is the planting of ideas," says Maathai. "By starting with the simple step of digging a hole and planting a tree, we plant hope for ourselves and for future generations."

We only need to capture one part in 10,000 of the sunlight that falls on the Earth to meet 100 percent of our energy needs. This will become feasible with nanoengineered solar panels and nanoengineered fuel cells.

RAY KURZWEIL, b. 1948, inventor and futurologist member of the U.S. National Academy of Engineering, February 2008

FAME

Famous men have the whole earth as their memorial.
PERICLES, c. 495–429 BC, Greek orator

I am the greatest!
MUHAMMAD ALI, b. 1942, American boxer

If you would not be forgotten as soon as you are dead, either write things worth reading or do things worth writing.

BENJAMIN FRANKLIN, 1706–1790, American writer, scientist, and diplomat

Celebrities are visible and essential **role models** in an age of moral disorientation. **David Beckham's** trip to Liberia in January 2008 as UNICEF ambassador highlighted the desperate issue of child mortality in the country. His wife, **Victoria,** is a champion of the Meningitis Research Foundation. **Bono** and **Bob Geldof** famously brought Africa's suffering to the world. **Bollywood stars** raised enormous funds for tsunami victims. **George Clooney** has been key in bringing the world's attention to the plight of Darfur.

Fame pays and pays well. No doubt about it! **Angelina Jolie,** apparently, picks up between $15 million and $20 million per film. **Nicole Kidman** can expect to earn up to $15 million.

Everything a human being wants can be divided into four components: love, adventure, power and fame.

JOHANN WOLFGANG VON GOETHE, 1749–1832, German writer

The desire for fame tempts even noble minds.

ST. AUGUSTINE, 354–430 AD, City of God

Andy Warhol said in the future everyone will be world-famous for fifteen minutes. That's probably a bit ambitious, but a contemporary American artist, **Raul Vincent Enriquez**, came up with a cunning plan called "I in the Sky," to give everyone **a minute of fame** by setting up a 2,500-square-foot screen in Times Square in New York. Portraits, taken from photo booths, were flashed up onto the screen for the public to see and admire.

FAMILY

No matter what you've done for yourself or for humanity, if you can't look back on having given love and attention to your own family, what have you really accomplished?
ELBERT HUBBARD, 1856–1915, American writer and philosopher

I do think that families are the most beautiful things in all the world!
LOUISA MAY ALCOTT, 1832–1888, spoken by Josephine "Jo" March in Little Women *(1868)*

The home we first knew on this beautiful earth,
The friends of our childhood, the place of our birth,
In the heart's inner chamber sung always will be,
As the shell ever sings of its home in the sea.
FRANCES DANA GAGE, *1808–1884, American social reformer*

The happiness of the domestic fireside is the first boon of Heaven; and it is well it is so, since it is that which is the lot of the mass of mankind.
THOMAS JEFFERSON, *1743–1826, third U.S. president*

Thy wife shall be as a fruitful vine by the sides of thine house: thy children like olive plants round about thy table.
Psalm 128:3

Article 16(3) of the Universal Declaration of Human Rights:

The family is the natural and fundamental group unit of society and is entitled to protection by society and the State.

I am the family face;
Flesh perishes, I live on,
Projecting trait and trace
Through time to times anon,
And leaping from place to place
Over oblivion.
THOMAS HARDY, *1840–1928, English writer, "Heredity"*

We cannot destroy kindred: our chains stretch a little sometimes, but they never break.

MARQUISE DE SÉVIGNÉ, 1626–1696, letter writer

FAMOUS LAST WORDS

Why not, why not, why not. Yeah.

TIMOTHY LEARY, 1920–1996, American writer

Am I dying, or is this my birthday?

NANCY ASTOR, 1879–1964, first female member of the British Parliament, upon seeing all her children at her bedside during her last illness

God will pardon me. It's his profession.

HEINRICH HEINE, 1797–1856, German poet

Don't pull down the blinds! I feel fine. I want the sunlight to greet me.

RUDOLPH VALENTINO, 1895–1926, Hollywood heartthrob

I shall hear in Heaven.

LUDWIG VAN BEETHOVEN, 1770–1827, German composer

I've just had eighteen straight scotches. I do believe that is a record.

DYLAN THOMAS, 1914–1953, Welsh poet

One day, when the going is tough and the big game is hanging in the balance, ask the team to win one for the Gipper. I don't know where I'll be, Rock, but I'll know about it and I'll be happy.

GEORGE GIPP, 1895–1920, legendary American football player, to his coach Knute Rockne

That was a great game of golf, fellers.

BING CROSBY, 1903–1977, American singer and actor

It's very beautiful over there.

THOMAS EDISON, 1847–1931, American inventor

Before drowning in the Lusitania, 1915:

Why fear death? It is the most beautiful adventure in life.

CHARLES FROHMAN, 1860–1915, American theatrical producer

Death is nothing, nor life either, for that matter. To die, to sleep, to pass into nothingness, what does it matter? Everything is an illusion.

MATA HARI, 1876–1917, Dutch courtesan and spy, before blowing her executioners a kiss

So the heart be right, it is no matter which way the head lies.

SIR WALTER RALEIGH, 1552–1618, Renaissance man, to his executioner

Why yes, a bullet-proof vest!

JAMES W. RODGERS, d. 1960, American criminal, when asked for his last request in front of the firing squad

FASHION

I believe that style is the only real luxury that is really desirable.

Attributed to GIORGIO ARMANI, b. 1934

The only rule is don't be boring and dress cute wherever you go. Life is too short to blend in.

Attributed to PARIS HILTON, b. 1981

I don't design clothes, I design dreams.

Attributed to RALPH LAUREN, b. 1939, New York Times, *APRIL 19, 1986*

A man with a good coat upon his back meets with a better reception than he who has a bad one.

SAMUEL JOHNSON, 1709–1784, English writer, quoted in James Boswell's The Life of Samuel Johnson

Recent excavations at Plocnik in Serbia, dating back 7,500 years, show that young women of the Serbian Neolithic tribes, wore short tops and miniskirts not dissimilar to those of today. Fashion was evidently an essential ingredient of being human even in prehistoric times.

In 2008 the burghers of Amsterdam began handing over the use of the city's infamous sex shop windows to fashion designers, replacing real women with plastic models dressed in the latest trendy styles. It is hoped that fashion will beat the area's reputation for debauchery, drugs, and crime.

All the rudiments of life are to be found ironing trousers.

CHRIS EUBANK, b. 1966, boxing champion, The Independent, *UK newspaper (2003)*

This bikini made me a success.

URSULA ANDRESS, b. 1936, Swiss actress

Fashion is not something that exists in dresses only. Fashion is in the sky, in the street, fashion has to do with ideas, the way we live, what is happening.

COCO CHANEL, 1883–1971, French fashion designer

I don't get out of bed for less than $10,000 a day.

LINDA EVANGELISTA, b. 1965, Canadian supermodel

FOOD

Edible, adj. Good to eat, and wholesome to digest, as a worm to a toad, a toad to a snake, a snake to a pig, a pig to a man, and a man to a worm.

AMBROSE BIERCE, 1842–c.1914, The Devil's Dictionary *(1911)*

This coffee falls into your stomach, and straightway there is a general commotion. Ideas begin to move like the battalions of the Grand Army of the battlefield, and the battle takes place. Things remembered arrive at full gallop, ensuing to the wind. The light cavalry of comparisons deliver a magnificent deploying charge, the artillery of logic hurry up with their train and ammunition, the shafts of imagination start up like sharpshooters. Similes arise, the paper is covered with ink; for the struggle commences and is concluded with torrents of black water, just as a battle with powder.

HONORÉ DE BALZAC, 1799–1850, "The Pleasures and Pains of Coffee"

Vegetarianism is harmless enough though it is apt to fill a man with wind and self-righteousness.

SIR ROBERT HUTCHISON, 1871–1960, president of the Royal College of Physicians

I am convinced digestion is the great secret to life.

SYDNEY SMITH, 1771–1845, English writer

The test of a cook is how she boils an egg. My boiled eggs are FANTASTIC, FABULOUS. Sometimes as hard as a 100 carat diamond, or again soft as a feather bed, or running like a cool stream, they can also burst like fireworks from their shells and take on the look and rubbery texture of a baby octopus. Never a dull egg, with me.

NANCY MITFORD, 1904–1973, English writer, in a letter dated October 1963

Nothing will benefit human health and increase the chances for survival of life on Earth as much as the evolution to a vegetarian diet.

ALBERT EINSTEIN, 1879–1955, German-born physicist

Organic farming can produce up to three times as much food as conventional farming in developing countries, according to a study published by leading U.S. researchers in 2007. Estimates based on 293 published studies on yields from organic farming show that organic methods could produce enough food to sustain the current human population, and potentially an even larger population, without expanding the agricultural land base.

To eat well in England all you have to do is take breakfast three times a day.

W. SOMERSET MAUGHAM, 1874–1965, English writer

I want there to be no peasant in my kingdom so poor that he is unable to have a chicken in his pot every Sunday.

HENRY IV, 1553–1610, king of France, at his coronation in 1589

The discovery of a new dish does more for human happiness than the discovery of a new star.

ANTHELME BRILLAT-SAVARIN, 1855–1926, French politician,
The Physiology of Taste

A man may be a pessimistic determinist before lunch and an optimistic believer in the will's freedom after it.

ALDOUS HUXLEY, 1894–1963, English novelist

FRIENDSHIP

A friend may well be reckoned the masterpiece of Nature.

RALPH WALDO EMERSON, 1803–1882, American essayist and poet

Song of the Young War God

I have been to the end of the earth.
I have been to the end of the waters.
I have been to the end of the sky.
I have been to the end of the mountains.
I have found none that were not my friends.
Traditional Navajo Song

The friends thou hast, and their adoption tried,
Grapple them to thy soul with hoops of steel . . .
WILLIAM SHAKESPEARE, Hamlet *(1602), advice from Polonius*
to his son

We have fewer friends than we imagine, but more than
we know.
HUGO VON HOFMANNSTHAL, *1874–1929, Austrian poet*

Seventy-four children aged between three and eight, half
of whom had a current or past imaginary friend, were
asked by **Dr. Paula Bouldin of Deakin University** about
the "mythical content" of their daydreams or game playing. The group with imaginary friends was shown to
have a far richer fantasy life than those without, with an
ability to "almost . . . see and hear the contents of their
daydream in front of them" says the report, published in
the **Journal of Genetic Psychology.**

Friendship is nothing else than entire fellow feeling as to
all things human and divine with mutual good-will and
affection; and I doubt whether anything better than this,
wisdom alone excepted, has been given to man by the
immortal gods.
CICERO, *106–43 BC, "On Friendship"*

As we all know, you can't choose your relatives, but you can choose your friends, and now studies have shown that you can more than get by with a little help from them. A longitudinal study of 1,500 people over the age of seventy at the **Centre for Ageing Studies at Flinders University in Adelaide, Australia,** revealed that, while close connections with children and other relatives had little to no effect on longevity, those with larger networks of friends and confidantes were 22 percent less likely to die over a ten-year follow-up period than those with smaller numbers of friends.

Friends are God's apology for relations.
HUGH KINGSMILL, 1889–1949, British writer

Am I not destroying my enemies when I make friends of them?
ABRAHAM LINCOLN, 1809–1865, U.S. president

Don't walk in front of me, I may not follow.
Don't walk behind me, I may not lead.
Walk beside me and be my friend.
ALBERT CAMUS, 1913–1960

FUTURE

Future, n. That period of time in which our affairs prosper, our friends are true and our happiness is assured.

AMBROSE BIERCE, 1842–c.1914, The Devil's Dictionary *(1911)*

I have seen the future, and it works.

LINCOLN STEFFENS, 1866–1936, American journalist

Don't worry about the world ending today. It's already tomorrow in Australia.

CHARLES M. SCHULZ, 1922–2000, American cartoonist

Many cultures believe in a cycle of destiny, in which mankind goes through successive stages, sometimes worse, sometimes better. Vedic writings refer to Golden (Satya), Silver (Treta), Bronze (Dwapara), and Iron (Kali) ages, which take their turns (of roughly three thousand years each) first descending and then ascending. So, with the Renaissance marking, roughly, the latest transition from Iron, we are now in an ascending Bronze Age, and will hit the early stages of the next Golden Age in around five thousand years' time.

A PREDICTION FROM LEO TOLSTOY (1828–1910):

I see the nations growing wiser and realising that the alluring woman of their destinies is nothing but an illusion after all. There will be a time when the world will have no use for armies, hypocritical religions, and degenerate art.

A Miss is as Good as Thousands of Miles

On January 7, 2002, a stadium-sized asteroid named 2001 YB5, big enough to wipe out an entire country, hurtled toward a rendezvous with Earth. Luckily, we had moved on a mere *four hours* earlier, and it missed us by just twice the distance of the Moon—a whisker in celestial terms. In the last seventy years or so, at least twenty-two asteroids are known to have come even closer than this one; in fact, for every object that does hit us, such as the 1908 Siberian asteroid, whose impact was six hundred times that of Hiroshima, tens of thousands miss, and one hundred tons worth are burned up in our atmosphere daily. Still more fortuitously, so far no object has ever hit a densely populated area. Meanwhile, "Apophis," a twenty-million ton asteroid homing in on us with a 1 in 45,000 chance that it could hit on April 13, 2036, is concentrating minds wonderfully. With the UN now taking the problem seriously, we look set to develop the means not only to locate and track such threats to our survival, but also, by using solutions such as a massive spacecraft as a "gravitational tractor," to divert them.

Humanity has the stars in its future, and that future is too important to be lost under the burden of juvenile folly and ignorant superstition.

ISAAC ASIMOV, 1920–1992, American author

It's not all stars and tea leaves. Here are a few other tried and tested techniques for divining the future:

Augury *(studying the flights or cries of birds)*

Capnomancy *(observing patterns in smoke)*

Chiromancy *(fortune-telling by the hand)*

Geloscopy *(watching the way somebody, usually a medium, laughs)*

Gyromancy *(divination by walking in a circle and falling down dizzy)*

Haruspication *(inspecting the entrails of animals)*

Myomancy *(observing the movement of mice)*

Necromancy *(questioning the spirits of the dead about the future)*

Oneiromancy *(divination by dreams)*

Scatoscopy *(examining excrement)*

Sortilege *(casting of lots)*

Spodomancy *(studying ashes)*

2012 . . . IS WHEN EVERYTHING BEGINS AGAIN

The ancient Mayans, who were great astronomers, had at least twenty different calendars, all of which were devilishly precise. That civilization is long gone, but their Long Count calendar, which has now been going for over five thousand years, continues, coming to an end on December 21, 2012. The Mayans held that this date was sacred and propitious, and it is still widely believed that this auspicious moment will herald the beginning of a new dawn for mankind.

GENIUS

What creates men of genius, or rather, what they create, is not new ideas, it is that idea—inside them—that what has been said has still not been said enough.

Eugène Delacroix, 1798–1863, Journal of Eugène Delacroix *(1824)*

A man of genius makes no mistakes.

James Joyce, 1882–1941, Irish writer, Ulysses *(1922)*

Neither a lofty degree of intelligence nor imagination nor both together go to the making of genius. Love, love, love, that is the soul of genius.

Wolfgang Amadeus Mozart, 1756–1791, Austrian composer

When you close your doors, and make darkness within, remember never to say that you are alone, for you are not alone; nay, God is within, and your genius is within. And what need have they of light to see what you are doing?

Epictetus, c.50–c.138 AD

Mediocrity knows nothing higher than itself, but talent instantly recognises genius.

Sir Arthur Conan Doyle, 1859–1930, The Valley of Fear *(1915)*

Genius is felt, but it is not imitated.

Denis Diderot, 1713–1784, Discours sur la poésie dramatique *(1758)*

An IQ of 140-plus is considered to be genius. Were the great men of history all geniuses? We have no way of knowing how they would have fared in an intelligence test, but it is safe to imagine that Voltaire, Bach, Beethoven, Kant, Cervantes, Darwin, Mozart, Spinoza, Michelangelo, Leonardo da Vinci, Isaac Newton, Blaise Pascal, and Ludwig Wittgenstein, for example, would have achieved high scores. Test your IQ online with www.iqtest.com or go straight to Mensa, the society for people with high IQs, and order your own IQ test form: www.mensa.org.

When a true genius appears in the world, you may know him by this sign, that the dunces are all in confederacy against him.

JONATHAN SWIFT, 1667–1745, Thoughts on Various Subjects *(1711)*

Yehudi Menuhin was a musical prodigy, a genius performing to audiences around the world at the age of thirteen. Mozart was already composing at age five. Rimbaud gave up on poetry aged nineteen having composed some of the most beautiful we know. As a teenager, Picasso would routinely draw pictures most of us wouldn't manage in a lifetime of trying!

Talent is like a marksman who hits a target that others cannot reach; genius is like the marksman who hits a target . . . others cannot even see.

ARTHUR SCHOPENHAUER, 1788–1860, German philosopher

Patience is a necessary ingredient of genius.

BENJAMIN DISRAELI, 1804–1881, Contarini Fleming

Any fool can make things bigger, more complex, and more violent. It takes a touch of genius—and a lot of courage—to move in the opposite direction.

JOHN DRYDEN, 1631–1700, Epistle X—To Congreve

Genius is an African who dreams up snow.

Attributed to VLADIMIR NABOKOV, 1899–1977, novelist

HEALTH

He who has health has hope; and he who has hope has everything.

Arabic proverb

We can close the books on infectious diseases.

WILLIAM H. STEWART, 1921–2008, surgeon general of the United States, addressing the U.S. Congress in 1969

I reckon being ill as one of the greatest pleasures of life, provided one is not too ill and is not obliged to work until one is better.

SAMUEL BUTLER, *1835–1902,* The Way of All Flesh *(1903)*

The art of medicine consists of amusing the patient while nature cures the disease.

VOLTAIRE, *1694–1778*

One should pray to have a sound mind in a sound body.

JUVENAL, *c.55–c.140,* Satirae

One finger in the throat and one in the rectum makes a good diagnostician.

SIR WILLIAM OSLER, *1849–1919, Canadian physician*

Causes for optimism occasioned by development of vaccines in recent times

Polio (1962)	Meningitis (1978)
Measles (1963)	Hepatitis B (1981)
Mumps (1967)	Hepatitis A (1992)
Rubella (1970)	Lyme disease (1998)
Chicken pox (1974)	Rotavirus (1998)
Pneumonia (1977)	Human papilloma virus (2006)

Keep up the spirits of your patient with the music of the viol and the psaltery, or by forging letters telling of the death of his enemies or (if he be a cleric) by informing that he has been made a bishop.

HENRI DE MONDEVILLE, 1260–1320, pioneering French surgeon

I have been accustomed for some time past, to apply leeches to the inflamed testicle, which practice has always been followed with most happy effects.

WILLIAM BUCHAN, 1729–1805, Domestic Medicine *(1798)*

A clown is like an aspirin, only he works twice as fast.

GROUCHO MARX, 1890–1977, American comedian

Unfounded Health Scares in 2004, Published by the American Council of Science & Health

Mobile phones cause brain tumors
Nightlights cause leukemia
MMR vaccines cause autism
PCBs in salmon cause cancer
Mercury in seafood causes neurological problems
Cheeseburgers caused Bill Clinton's cardiovascular disease
Antibiotics cause breast cancer
Teflon causes health problems in humans
Fizzy drinks cause esophageal cancer

HISTORY

What is all Knowledge too but recorded experience, and a product of history; of which, therefore, reasoning and belief, no less than action and passion, are essential materials?

THOMAS CARLYLE, 1795–1881, Scottish essayist

His Majesty's government favors the establishment in Palestine of a national home for the Jewish people, and will use their best endeavors to facilitate the advancement of this object, it being clearly understood that nothing shall be done which may prejudice the civil and religious rights of existing non-Jewish communities in Palestine, or the rights and political status enjoyed by Jews in any other country.

BALFOUR DECLARATION, November 2, 1917

. . . But unquestionably there never was a time in the history of this country when, from the situation of Europe, we might more reasonably expect fifteen years of peace, than we may at the present moment.

PRIME MINISTER WILLIAM PITT in a speech in the House of Commons, February 17, 1792. Britain entered into the First Coalition against France later that year and was either at war, or on a war footing with her, until Waterloo in 1815.

If history were taught in the form of stories, it would never be forgotten.
RUDYARD KIPLING, 1865–1936, English author

The past is the only dead thing that smells sweet.
EDWARD THOMAS, 1878–1917, English poet

The real triumph is that it has shown that representatives of four great Powers can find it possible to agree on a way of carrying out a difficult and delicate operation by discussion instead of by force of arms, and thereby they have averted a catastrophe which would have ended civilization as we have known it . . . After everything that has been said about the German Chancellor [Hitler] today and in the past, I do feel that the House ought to recognize the difficulty for a man in that position to take back such emphatic declarations as he had already made amidst the enthusiastic cheers of his supporters, and to recognize that in consenting, even though it were only at the last moment, to discuss with the representatives of other Powers those things which he had declared he had already decided once for all, was a real and a substantial contribution on his part. With regard to Signor Mussolini . . . I think that Europe and the world have reason to be grateful to the head of the Italian government for his work in contributing to a peaceful solution.

PRIME MINISTER NEVILLE CHAMBERLAIN in defense of Munich agreement in House of Commons 1938

HUMAN NATURE

There are many wonderful things, and nothing is more wonderful than man.

SOPHOCLES, c. 496–406 BC, Greek playwright

For man, the vast marvel is to be alive. For man, as for flower and beast and bird, the supreme triumph is to be most vividly, most perfectly alive. Whatever the unborn and the dead may know, they cannot know the beauty, the marvel of being alive in the flesh. The dead may look after the afterwards. But the magnificent here and now of life in the flesh is ours, and ours alone, and ours only for a time. We ought to dance with rapture that we should be alive and in the flesh, and part of the living, incarnate cosmos.

D. H. LAWRENCE, 1885–1930, English writer, Apocalypse (1930)

There is surely a piece of divinity in us, something that was before the elements, and owes no homage unto the sun.

SIR THOMAS BROWNE, 1605–1682, English philosopher

Is man an ape or an angel? Now I am on the side of the angels.

BENJAMIN DISRAELI, 1804–1881, British statesman

Dr. Martin Seligman, the founder of Positive Psychology, has proven through research that it is possible to be happier, regardless of one's circumstances. To that end, the *Character Strengths and Virtues* handbook, which identifies the positive psychological traits of human beings, has been developed. In a nutshell, they are: Wisdom and Knowledge; Courage; Humanity; Justice; Temperance; and Transcendence. Find out more about the University of Pennsylvania Positive Psychology Center, and participate in ongoing research into improving the human condition, at www.authentichappiness.sas.upenn.edu.

If you feel that life, however wonderful, could be even better, why not join the Transhumanist movement? The aim is to use technology to improve on the basic human model, thereby eliminating such things as suffering, disease, old age and, eventually, involuntary death. In 1998, the World Transhumanist Association, dedicated to a continuous improvement in the human condition and a strongly optimistic view of future advances to ameliorate the human lot, was set up. If you believe that body modification, cybernetics, nanotechnology, and bioengineering are the way forward, and would like to consciously help humanity to evolve, go to www.transhumanism.org or to the website of The Extropy Institute, www.extropy.org, where you can volunteer to test new technology, possibly allowing for radical human enhancement by the middle of this century.

Man, unlike any other thing organic or inorganic in the universe, grows beyond his work, walks up the stairs of his concepts, emerges ahead of his accomplishments.

JOHN STEINBECK, 1902–1968, The Grapes of Wrath *(1939)*

But we were born of risen apes, not fallen angels, and the apes were armed killers besides. And so what shall we wonder at? Our murders and massacres and missiles, and our irreconcilable regiments? Or our treaties whatever they may be worth; our symphonies, however seldom they may be played; our peaceful acres, however frequently they may be converted into battlefields; our dreams, however rarely they may be accomplished. The miracle of man is not how far he has sunk but how magnificently he has risen. We are known among the stars by our poems, not our corpses.

ROBERT ARDREY, 1908–1980, American anthropologist,
African Genesis *(1961)*

KINDNESS

No act of kindness, no matter how small, is ever wasted.
AESOP, 620–560 BC

We are made for co-operation, like feet, like hands, like eyelids, like the rows of the upper and lower teeth. To act against one another is contrary to nature.

MARCUS AURELIUS, 121–180, Roman emperor and philosopher

The best way to begin a day well might be to think on waking whether one can give pleasure to at least one person. If this could become a substitute for the religious habit of prayer, our fellow-men would benefit.

FRIEDRICH NIETZSCHE, 1844–1900, Human, All-Too-Human (1878)

Random Acts of Kindness Week is in February, and World Kindness Week is every November: www.actsofkindness.org. What goes around, comes around.

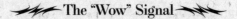

The "Wow" Signal

In 1977, Dr. Jerry Ehman, of Ohio State University, picked up a startlingly strong radio signal with the Big Ear radio telescope and scribbled "WOW!" in the margin of the computer printout. It is the most likely candidate for an artificial signal—in other words, news from elsewhere—ever discovered, but it has not been detected since. Yet the search for extraterrestrial intelligence goes on. Researchers have been combing the skies for radio signals from aliens for nearly fifty years. The SETI Institute (the Search for Extraterrestrial Intelligence) was set up over twenty years ago, and by 2028, it's estimated that SETI will have combed more than a million star systems, looking for intergalactic friends.

Whenever there is a human being there is an opportunity for kindness.

SENECA, c. 4 BC–AD 59, Roman Stoic philosopher

I expect to pass through this world but once; any good thing therefore that I can do, or any kindness that I can show to any fellow-creature, let me do it now, let me not defer or neglect it, for I shall not pass this way again.

Stephen Grellet, 1773–1855, Quaker missionary

I always prefer to believe the best of everybody—it saves so much trouble.

Rudyard Kipling, 1865–1936, English author

LAW & LAWYERS

The people should fight for the law as for their city wall.

Heraclitus, Greek philosopher

We hold these truths to be self-evident, that all men are created equal, that they are endowed by their Creator with certain unalienable rights, that among these are life, liberty and the pursuit of happiness.

Preamble to U.S. Declaration of Independence, 1776

Reason is the life of the law, nay the common law itself is nothing else but reason . . . The law, which is the perfection of reason.

Sir Edward Coke, 1552–1634, English jurist

The English constitution has in fact arrived at the point of excellence, in consequence of which all men are restored to those natural rights of which in nearly all monarchies they are deprived. These rights are: total liberty of person and property; freedom of the press; the right of trial in all criminal cases by an independent jury; the right of being tried only according to the strict letter of the law; and the right of each man to profess any religion he desires.

VOLTAIRE, 1694–1778, Dictionnaire Philosophique

Pressure of opinion a hundred years ago brought about the emancipation of the slaves. It is now for man to insist upon the same freedom for his mind as he has won for his body.

Lawyer PETER BENENSON, article in The Observer *entitled "The Forgotten Prisoners," launching Appeal for Amnesty, later to be known as Amnesty International*

It may be true that the law cannot make a man love me, but it can keep him from lynching me, and I think that's pretty important.

MARTIN LUTHER KING JR., 1929–1968, civil rights activist

. . . Recognition of the inherent dignity and of the equal and inalienable rights of all members of the human family is the foundation of freedom, justice and peace in the world.

Preamble to the Universal Declaration of Human Rights, 1948

LIFE

There is no wealth but life.

JOHN RUSKIN, 1819–1900, English author and poet

There's night and day, brother, both sweet things; sun, moon, and stars, brother, all sweet things; there's likewise a wind on the heath. Life is very sweet, brother; who would wish to die?

GEORGE BORROW, 1803–1881, English author, Lavengro *(1851)*

LIFE IS:

. . . a pure flame, and we live by an invisible Sun within us.

SIR THOMAS BROWNE, 1605–1682, English author

. . . the art of drawing sufficient conclusions from insufficient premises.

SAMUEL BUTLER, 1835–1902, English novelist

. . . colour and warmth and light
And a striving evermore for these . . .

JULIAN GRENFELL, 1888–1915, English poet, "Into Battle"

The mere sense of living is joy enough.

EMILY DICKINSON, 1830–1886, American poet

December 22, 1912

Palaeontology has its comfortable words too. I have revelled in my littleness and irresponsibility. It has relieved me of the harassing desire to live, I feel content to live dangerously, indifferent to my fate; I have discovered I am a fly, that we are all flies, that nothing matters. It's a great load off my life, for I don't mind being such a microorganism—to me the honour is sufficient of belonging to the universe—such a great universe, so grand a scheme of things. Not even Death can rob me of that honour. For nothing can alter the fact that I have lived; I have been I, if for ever so short a time.

W. N. P. Barbellion, 1889–1919, British naturalist, Journal of a Disappointed Man *(1919)*

I slept and dreamed that life was joy,
I awoke and saw that life was duty,
I acted, and behold duty was joy.

Rabindranath Tagore, 1861–1941, winner of the 1913 Nobel Prize for Literature

Pleasure is the beginning and the goal of a happy life.
Epicurus, 341–270 BC, Greek philosopher

Is it so small a thing to have enjoyed the sun,
To have lived light in the spring,
To have loved,
To have thought,
To have done?

Matthew Arnold, 1822–1888, "The Hymn of Empedocles" (1852)

If you feel that life is one of God's jokes, there is still no reason why we shouldn't make it a *good* joke.

KENNETH WILLIAMS, 1926–1988, British actor

LOVE

There is only one happiness in life, to love and be loved.

GEORGE SAND, 1804–1876, French author

LOVE

. . . is a fruit in season at all times, and within reach of every hand.

MOTHER TERESA, 1910–1997, Catholic missionary

. . . is one soul inhabiting two bodies.

ARISTOTLE, 384–322 BC

. . . is someone you can be silly with.

CECIL BEATON, 1904–1980, photographer

I shall show you a love philtre compounded without drug or herb or witches' spell. It is this: if you wish to be loved, love.

HECATO, c. 100 BC, Stoic philosopher

The Meaning of Love

Those four letters, L-O-V-E, contain multitudes. The Ancient Greeks used three different words in place of our catch-all one: *Agape*, the love that people have for God, duty, or family; *Philia*, which denoted the love we feel for friends; and *Eros*, love for a lover.

The simple act of falling in love is as beneficial as it is astonishing.

ROBERT LOUIS STEVENSON, *1850–1894, Scottish writer*

Man has bought brains, but all the millions in the world have failed to buy love. Man has subdued bodies, but all the power on earth has been unable to subdue love. Man has conquered whole nations, but all his armies could not conquer love. Man has chained and fettered the spirit, but he has been utterly helpless before love. High on a throne, with all the splendor and pomp his gold can command, man is yet poor and desolate, if love passes him by. And if it stays, the poorest hovel is radiant with warmth, with life and color. Thus love has the magic power to make of a beggar a king.

EMMA GOLDMAN, *1869–1940, anarchist, "Marriage and Love,"* in Anarchism and Other Essays *(1911)*

If I can't love Hitler, I can't love at all.

REV. A. J. MUSTE, *1885–1967, American pacifist, at a Quaker meeting in 1940*

According to proverbial wisdom
from all around the world, Love:

makes the world go round; will find a way; teaches even donkeys to dance; sees roses without thorns; pays no attention to dignity; makes the impossible possible; rules without rules; makes labor light; laughs at locksmiths; can be neither bought nor sold; rules his kingdom without a sword; understands all languages; conquers all; is as strong as death.

How do I love thee? Let me count the ways.

I Love thee to the depth and breadth and height
My soul can reach, when feeling out of sight
For the ends of Being and ideal Grace.
I love thee to the level of everyday's
Most quiet need, by sun and candlelight.
I love thee freely, as men strive for Right;
I love thee purely, as they turn from Praise.
I love thee with the passion put to use
In my old griefs, and with my childhood's faith.
I love thee with a love I seemed to lose
With my lost saints,—I love thee with the breath,
Smiles, tears, of all my life!—and, if God choose,
I shall but love thee better after death.
ELIZABETH BARRETT BROWNING, 1806–1861, English poet,
Sonnets from the Portuguese *(1850)*

MARRIAGE

IT MUST BE LOVE

The *Harian Metro* newspaper in Malaysia recently reported that a thirty-three-year-old man from the north of the country has married a 104-year-old woman. It is the man's first marriage and the bride's twenty-first. Muhamad, an ex-army serviceman, declared that he had found peace and a strong sense of belonging after meeting Wook Kundor. The groom went on to say that he couldn't be accused of going after his wife's money as she had none.

Who said Iranian women were oppressed? A wife in Iran has managed to have her husband condemned for his avarice in a court of law. The stingy husband was ordered to buy 124,000 red roses for his wife. The court seized the man's apartment until all the roses appeared.

As reported in the Iranian daily, Etemad.

There is no more lovely, friendly and charming relationship, communion or company than a good marriage.

MARTIN LUTHER, *1483–1546, German theologian*

Marriage Is Good For You

According to Professor Andrew Oswald, of Warwick University, "the singleton life is seriously bad for your health and can be almost as bad as smoking," while the wedded life actually boosts the immune system. If that's a bit too vague, research presented to the American Psychosomatic Society shows that, if you're happily married, cuts and grazes are likely to heal more quickly. Researchers monitored forty-two couples and found that their (medically induced) minor wounds healed almost twice as fast among those happily married than among those less so.

Marriage is the result of the longing for the deep, deep peace of the double bed after the hurly-burly of the chaise-longue.

MRS. PATRICK CAMPBELL, 1865–1940, British stage actress

. . . In what stupid age or nation
Was marriage ever out of fashion?
SAMUEL BUTLER, 1612–1680, English poet

Man's best possession is a sympathetic wife.

EURIPIDES, 484–406 BC, Antigone

The **Virgin Islands,** ironically, is the place with the highest marriage rate in the world.

There was an old man from Orissa . . . Eighty-year-old Udaynath Dakshiniray, from India, has had ninety wives and twenty-nine children. All his ninety wives were from impoverished families and, before tying the knot, he presented each one with at least five acres of land. The *Asian Age* reports that when asked why he had married so often, Dakshiniray said he was on a social mission to help women overcome social stigma and harassment. He had started out in life with over four hundred acres of land and others weren't as fortunate as he. Udaynath Dakshiniray intends to carry on marrying. In fact, he claims to have recently received nine offers of marriage from abroad, from the United States, Japan, Hungary, and Germany. Serial monogamy as social service—could it catch on?

Marriage, it has been proven, makes men more successful and richer. The 10 to 40 percent wage premium married men receive compared to their unmarried counterparts is in fact "one of the most well-documented phenomena in social science."

Sir Temulji Bhicaji Nariman and Lady Nariman, from India, and Lazarus Rowe and Molly Webber, from the United States, share the world record for the longest marriage: eighty-six years. According to records, the oldest couple ever to wed was François Fernandez, aged ninety-six, and Madeleine Francineau, aged ninety-four, in 2002.

MEDIA

I think it's fair to say that personal computers have become the most empowering tool we've ever created. They're tools of communication, they're tools of creativity, and they can be shaped by their user.

BILL GATES, b. 1955, American businessman

Let me make the newspapers, and I care not what is preached in the pulpit or what is enacted in Congress.

WENDELL PHILLIPS, 1811–1862, American abolitionist and orator

The BBC World Service is perhaps Britain's greatest gift to the world this century.

KOFI ANNAN, b. 1938, UN secretary-general, in 1999

The printing press is the greatest weapon in the armoury of the modern commander.

T. E. LAWRENCE, 1888–1935, British soldier and writer

It's not that the world has got much worse, just that the news coverage has got so much better.

Often attributed to G. K. CHESTERTON, 1874–1936

In these times we fight for ideas, and newspapers are our fortresses.

HEINRICH HEINE, 1797–1856, German poet and writer

Here is the living disproof of the old adage that nothing is as dead as yesterday's newspaper . . . This is what really happened, reported by a free press to a free people. It is the raw material of history; it is the story of our own times.

HENRY STEELE COMMAGER, 1902–1998, *historian*

Most of us probably feel we couldn't be free without newspapers, and that is the real reason we want the newspapers to be free.

EDWARD R. MURROW, 1908–1965, *broadcast journalist*

The pen is mightier than the sword.

EDWARD BULWER-LYTTON, 1803–1873, *English writer and politician*

Were it left to me to decide whether we should have a government without newspapers, or newspapers without a government, I should not hesitate a moment to prefer the latter.

THOMAS JEFFERSON, 1743–1826

Every time a newspaper dies, even a bad one, the country moves a little closer to authoritarianism; when a great one goes, like the *New York Herald Tribune*, history itself is denied a devoted witness.

RICHARD KLUGER, *b. 1934, Pulitzer Prize–winning author*

MEN

One machine can do the work of fifty ordinary men.
No machine can do the work of one extraordinary man.

ELBERT HUBBARD, 1856–1915, American writer and philosopher

Men are like wine. Some turn to vinegar, but the best
improve with age.

POPE JOHN XXIII, "The Good Pope," 1881–1963

In 1974, Janet Saltzman Chafetz, a sociology professor at the
University of Houston, pinpointed the following **Seven Areas
of Masculinity:**

1 Physical—virile, athletic, strong, brave. Unconcerned
   about appearance and aging

2 Functional—breadwinner, provider for family as much
   as mate

3 Sexual—sexually aggressive, experienced. Single status
   acceptable

4 Emotional—unemotional, stoic, the proverb says *Boys
   don't cry*

5 Intellectual—logical, intellectual, rational, objective,
   practical

6 Interpersonal—leader, dominating; disciplinarian;
   independent, free, individualistic; demanding

7 Other personal characteristics—success-oriented,
   ambitious, aggressive, proud, egotistical; moral, trust-
   worthy; decisive, competitive, uninhibited, adventurous

Men build bridges and throw railroads across deserts, and yet they contend successfully that the job of sewing on a button is beyond them. Accordingly, they don't have to sew buttons.

HEYWOOD BROUN, 1888–1939, American journalist, Seeing Things at Night *(1921)*

We're more proficient than women at arm wrestling, fresco-painting, ice hockey and particle physics. We make better cabinets, sun decks and booster rockets. We know how to read a map. In the movies, most Westerns and martial arts films would be poorer without our presence. . . . So let's renew our male mission and wear our antlers high on our heads. Let's stand up straight, aim well, and exercise our prerogative to leave the seat up. After all, we're MEN, and we hold a proud heritage in our hands.

RICK BAYAN, b. 1950, at the Cynic's Sanctuary, January 1999

The ManKind Project

For those who have lost or are still looking for their masculinity, the ManKind Project promotes "accountability and integrity; connection to feelings; leadership, fatherhood; and the blessing of elders". Join more than forty thousand men worldwide who have participated in its primary training, the New Warrior Training Adventure, at www.mkp.org.

A table, a chair, a bowl of fruit and a violin; what else does a man need to be happy?

ALBERT EINSTEIN, 1879–1955, German-born physicist

MIDDLE AGE

You don't understand life any better at forty than twenty, but you know it and you admit it. That's youth.

JULES RENARD, 1864–1910, French author

Forty is the old age of youth, fifty is the youth of old age.

VICTOR HUGO, 1802–1885, French poet

At twenty years of age, the will reigns, at thirty, the wit; at forty, the judgment.

BENJAMIN FRANKLIN, 1706–1790, Poor Richard's Almanac *(1758)*

At fifty you have the choice of keeping your face or your figure and it's much better to keep your face.

DAME BARBARA CARTLAND, 1901–2000, Daily Mail *(1981)*

I want to retire at fifty. I want to play cricket in the summer and geriatric football in the winter, and sing in the choir.

NEIL KINNOCK, b. 1942, The London Times, *July 28, 1980*

Lady Bracknell: Thirty-five is a very attractive age. London society is full of women of the very highest birth who have, of their own free choice, remained thirty-five for years.

OSCAR WILDE, 1854–1900, The Importance of Being Earnest *(1895)*

Women are most fascinating between the ages of thirty-five and forty, after they have won a few races and know how to pace themselves. Since few women ever pass forty, maximum fascination can continue indefinitely.

Attributed to CHRISTIAN DIOR, 1905–1957, Collier's Magazine, *June 10, 1955*

MIDDLE EAST

I believe it's going to happen, that there will be a signed peace treaty by the time I leave office. I am confident that with proper help the state of Palestine will emerge.

GEORGE W. BUSH, b. 1946, January 2008, press conference

Oil in the Middle East is the source of extraordinary wealth. Kuwait had an income of **$53.5 billion** last year. Iran is currently expecting oil revenues to hit **$60 billion.**

Algebra was named after Muslim scholar Al-Khwarizmi's 825 AD book, *Al-Jabr wa-al-Muqabilah*.

On Tuesday night I gave the order for British forces to take part in military action in Iraq. Tonight, British servicemen and women are engaged from air, land and sea. Their mission: to remove Saddam Hussein from power, and disarm Iraq of its weapons of mass destruction. I know this course of action has produced deep divisions of opinion in our country. But I know also the British people will now be united in sending our armed forces our thoughts and prayers. They are the finest in the world and their families and all of Britain can have great pride in them. The threat to Britain today is not that of my father's generation. War between the big powers is unlikely. Europe is at peace. The Cold War already a memory. But this new world faces a new threat: of disorder and chaos born either of brutal states like Iraq, armed with weapons of mass destruction; or of extreme terrorist groups. Both hate our way of life, our freedom, our democracy.

Tony Blair, b. 1953, March 21, 2003, prime minister's address

Damascus, Jerusalem, the Pyramids, the Sinai, Petra, Mecca, Mesopotamia, you name it, the Middle East is the cradle of human civilization. From here came Judaism, Christianity, and Islam and many of the pillars of Western and world society. The Sumerians are thought to have created the earliest human civilization over seven thousand years ago. They also invented the first hieroglyphs that became cuneiform, again possibly the oldest known written form of language. Jericho is the first known city of the world.

MUSIC

Music is Love in search of a word.

SIDNEY LANIER, 1842–1881, The Symphony *(1875)*

In early 2008, the Beatles' song **Across the Universe** was broadcast in space by NASA toward the star Polaris and became the first music sent into orbit. As well as aiming to connect with aliens, the purpose was to mark NASA's fiftieth anniversary.

The term **Mozart Effect** was first used to depict a supposed increase in brain activity and development that occurs when young children hear Mozart. It has entered common usage to describe the beneficial effects of music on all ages, from education to relaxation. Practitioners of **music therapy** believe, in fact, that music helps people with sensory and learning difficulties, neurological disabilities, and/or mental problems. It can be effective, it is further believed, in addressing behavioral and emotional issues, by focusing the body on motor functions, awareness, expression, and memory mechanisms. Studies at the American Association for the Advancement of Science, at Brown University, certainly back the belief that music can help construct emotional and intellectual abilities and reinforce children's academic skills.

Music is the universal language of mankind.
HENRY WADSWORTH LONGFELLOW, *1807–1882*, Outre Mer
(1835)

If the king loves music, there is little wrong in the land.
MENG-TZU, *c. 371–c. 289 BC, Chinese sage,* Discourses

The West-Eastern Divan was created by Daniel Barenboim and the late Edward Said. It brings together musicians from Israel, Palestine, and various Arab states. It uses music as enjoyment and fulfillment, but also as a way to bridge gaps between cultures and peoples, sharing knowledge and group work. In a similar way, and in an effort to ease tense relations with a country identified by George W. Bush as belonging to the Axis of Evil, America's oldest orchestra, the New York Philharmonic, stayed two days in North Korea, playing to packed audiences and standing ovations.

Music is a higher revelation than all wisdom and philosophy.
LUDWIG VAN BEETHOVEN, *1770–1827*

Music is life, and, like it, inextinguishable.
CARL AUGUST NIELSEN, *1865–1931*, Symphony No. 4 *(1916)*

Without music, life would be a mistake.
FRIEDRICH NIETZSCHE, *1844–1900*, Twilight of the Idols,
translated by R. J. Hollingdale (1889)

Top Optimistic Songs!

- "I Will Survive"—Gloria Gaynor
- "Reasons to be Cheerful 123"—Ian Dury and The Blockheads
- "All You Need Is Love"—The Beatles
- "Don't Worry Be Happy"—Bobby McFerrin
- "Singin' in the Rain"—Gene Kelly
- "Keep on the Sunny Side"—Ada Blenkhorn
- "Imagine"—John Lennon
- "You'll Never Walk Alone"—Rodgers & Hammerstein
- "Somewhere Over the Rainbow"—Harold Arlen, E. Y. Harburg
- "On the Sunny Side of the Street"—Dorothy Fields

NATURE

In Nature's inventions nothing is lacking, and nothing is superfluous.

LEONARDO DA VINCI, 1452–1519, Italian inventor and artist

We are so fond of being out in Nature, because it has no opinions about us.

FRIEDRICH NIETZSCHE, 1844–1900, Human, All-Too-Human (1878)

I love Nature partly because she is not man, but a retreat from him. None of his institutions control or pervade her. There a different kind of right prevails. In her midst I can be glad with an entire gladness. If this world were all man, I could not stretch myself, I should lose all hope. He is constraint, she is freedom to me. He makes me wish for another world. She makes me content with this.

HENRY DAVID THOREAU, *1817–1862*, Diary, *January 3, 1853*

There is a pleasure in the pathless woods,
There is a rapture on the lonely shore,
There is society, where none intrudes,
By the deep sea, and music in its roar:
I love not man the less, but nature more.
LORD BYRON, *1788–1824*, "Childe Harold's Pilgrimage" *(1812)*

Summer in the mountains
Too lazy to shift my white feather fan
I lie naked in the green woods.
Hanging my hat on a rock,
I bare my head to the breeze in the pines.
LI PO, *c.701–762 AD, Chinese poet*

I believe a leaf of grass is no less than the journey-work of the stars,
And the pismire is equally perfect, and a grain of sand, and the egg
  of the wren,
And the tree toad is a chef-d'oeuvre for the highest,
And the running blackberry would adorn the parlours of heaven.
  WALT WHITMAN, *1819–1892*, "Song of Myself" *(1855)*

Nature's Gift to Us

Current annual world energy use is 4.5×10^{20} joules, and a massive amount of that energy—some three-quarters of it—comes from burning fossil fuels. But the current annual energy poured down on the Earth from the sun is $3,000,000 \times 10^{20}$ joules—about 7,000 times as much energy as we currently use, totally free! And, with radical new ideas coming thick and fast, there is every reason to hope that we will soon find the tools to harness this extraordinary source of power.

OLD AGE

As I grow older, I constantly learn more.
SOLON, c. 640–c. 559 BC

Strength and beauty are the blessings of youth;
Temperance, however, is the flower of old age.
DEMOCRITUS, c. 460–c. 370 BC

To me old age is always fifteen years older than I am.
BERNARD MANNES BARUCH, 1870–1965, Newsweek, *August 29, 1955*

Well, there's no help for it. Ageing seems to be the only available way to live a long time.
DANIEL-FRANÇOIS-ESPRIT AUBER, 1782–1871

I do not think seventy years is the time of a man or woman,
Nor that seventy million years is the time of a man or woman,
Nor that years will ever stop the existence of me, or any one else.
WALT WHITMAN, 1819–1892, Leaves of Grass *(1855)*

The Abkhasia, a people who live in the Caucasus, claim to have elders living up to 150 years. Their secret: a lot of exercise (mountain climbing) and raw food such as nuts. The Hunza, who live in North Pakistan, also have mythical status for eternal youth. Their secret: fresh mountain air, exercise, and a diet based almost exclusively on fresh plants and fruits, which they grow themselves.

A man's only as old as the woman he feels.
GROUCHO MARX, 1890–1977, American comedian

No man loves life like him that's growing old.
SOPHOCLES, 496–406 BC

You are not necessarily your calendar or birth age. You might be eighty years old and in fact be sixty-five biologically. To test your real age, go to www.realage.com

It is erroneously believed that sexual activity lessens in old age. Not so. Intimate research coming out of Australia and America shows that many old-age pensioners carry on enjoying **sexual fulfillment** even into their nineties.

Jeanne Calment from Arles, South of France, remains the oldest documented person to have lived. She died in 1997 at the ripe old age of 122. She was riding a bicycle at one hundred and met Vincent Van Gogh when she was fourteen. She went to Victor Hugo's funeral in 1885. She once famously remarked: "I've only got one wrinkle and I'm sitting on it."

ORDER

Order is Heaven's first law.
ALEXANDER POPE, 1688–1744, "An Essay on Man" (1733)

A place for everything and everything in its place.
MRS. BEETON, 1836–1865, The Book of Household Management *(1861)*

Be regular and orderly in your life, so that you may be violent and original in your work.
GUSTAVE FLAUBERT, 1821–1880, French novelist

You're free. And freedom is beautiful. And, you know, it'll take time to restore chaos and order—order out of chaos. But we will.

GEORGE W. BUSH, b. 1946, U.S. president, 2003

We can form a precise idea of order, but not of disorder. Beauty, virtue, happiness, all have their proportions; ugliness, vice and unhappiness have none.

JACQUES-HENRI BERNADIN DE SAINT-PIERRE, 1737–1814, French writer and botanist, Paul et Virginie (1788)

Good order is the foundation of all good things.

EDMUND BURKE, 1729–1797, Reflections on the Revolution in France (1790)

The sacred formula of positivism: love as a principle, order as foundation, progress as goal.

AUGUSTE COMTE, 1798–1857, French thinker

Man is all symmetry
Full of proportions, one limb to another

GEORGE HERBERT, 1593–1633, "Man," from The Temple, Sacred Poems, and Private Ejaculations (1633)

I have been a rock of order.

PRINCE METTERNICH, 1773–1859, Austrian politician

PARENTHOOD

Trust yourself. You know more than you think you do.
DR. BENJAMIN SPOCK, 1903–1998, Baby and Child Care, *opening words (1955)*

For the hand that rocks the cradle
Is the hand that rules the world.
WILLIAM ROSS WALLACE, 1819–1881, *American poet*

The mother's yearning, that completest type of the life in another life which is the essence of real human love, feels the presence of the cherished child even in the debased, degraded man.
GEORGE ELIOT, 1819–1880, *English novelist,* Adam Bede *(1859)*

A *Time* poll conducted in December 2004 asked participants: "What one thing in life has brought you the greatest happiness?" Thirty-five percent said it was their children or grandchildren or both.

When I was a boy of fourteen, my father was so ignorant I could hardly stand to have the old man around. But when I got to be twenty-one, I was astonished at how much the old man had learned in seven years.
Attributed to MARK TWAIN, 1835–1910, *American humorist*

And a woman who held a babe against her bosom said, "Speak to us of Children." And he said:

Your children are not your children.
They are the sons and daughters of Life's longing for itself.
They come through you but not from you,
And though they are with you yet they belong not to you.

You may give them your love but not your thoughts,
For they have their own thoughts.
You may house their bodies but not their souls,
For their souls dwell in the house of tomorrow,
Which you cannot visit, not even in your dreams.
You may strive to be like them,
But seek not to make them like you.
For life goes not backward nor tarries with yesterday.

You are the bows from which your children
As living arrows are sent forth.
The archer sees the mark upon the path of the infinite,
And He bends you with His might
That His arrows may go swift and far.
Let your bending in the archer's hand be for gladness;
For even as He loves the arrow that flies,
So he loves also the bow that is stable.

KAHLIL GIBRAN, *1883–1931, Lebanese–American author,*
The Prophet *(1932)*

PATRIOTISM

A moment comes, which comes but rarely in history, when we step out from the old to the new, when an age ends, and when the sound of a nation, long suppressed, finds utterance.
JAWAHARLAL NEHRU, 1889–1964, Indian nationalist leader

I only regret that I have but one life to lose for my country.
NATHAN HALE, 1755–1776, American patriot, prior to execution by British for spying in 1776

Is it an offence, is it a mistake, is it a crime to take a hopeful view of the prospects of your own country? Why should it be? Why should patriotism and pessimism be identical? Hope is the mainspring of patriotism.
DAVID LLOYD GEORGE, 1863–1945, prime minister, British House of Commons

How sweet and fitting it is to die for one's country.
HORACE, 65–8 BC, Roman poet

Patriotism is a lively sense of collective responsibility. Nationalism is a silly cock crowing on his own dunghill.
RICHARD ALDINGTON, 1892–1962, The Colonel's Daughter (1931)

Be England what she will,
With all her faults, she is my country still.
CHARLES CHURCHILL, 1731–1764, "The Farewell" (1764)

Standing as I do in the view of God and eternity, I realize that patriotism is not enough. I must have no hatred or bitterness towards anyone.

EDITH CAVELL, 1865–1915, nurse, to the chaplain before her execution by German firing squad in 1915

POLITICS

A small body of determined spirits fired by an unquenchable faith in their mission can alter the course of history.

MAHATMA GANDHI, 1869–1948, Indian political and spiritual leader

We enter into a covenant that we shall build a society in which all South Africans, both black and white, will be able to walk tall, without fear in their hearts, assured of their inalienable right to human dignity—a rainbow nation at peace with itself and the world.

NELSON MANDELA, South African president, inaugural address, 1994

Politics is the art of the possible.
OTTO VON BISMARCK, 1815–1898

Top five of a 2007 Gallup poll
asking Americans who they regarded
as the country's greatest president:

Abraham Lincoln (18%)

Ronald Reagan (16%)

John F. Kennedy (14%)

Bill Clinton (13%)

Franklin Roosevelt (9%)

What are the Bolsheviki? They are the representatives of the most democratic government in Europe . . . Let us recognize the truest democracy in the world today.

WILLIAM RANDOLPH HEARST, 1863–1951, American newspaper magnate

With malice toward none; with charity for all; with firmness in the right, as God gives us to see the right, let us strive on to finish the work we are in.

ABRAHAM LINCOLN, 1809–1865, second inaugural address

We in America today are nearer to the final triumph over poverty than ever before in the history of any land.

HERBERT HOOVER, 1874–1964, during his 1928 election campaign. Within months, the worst crash in stock market history triggered the Great Depression.

Five Optimistic U.S. Election Pledges

Woodrow Wilson vows to keep the U.S. out of First World War

Franklin Roosevelt vows to keep the U.S. out of Second World War

Lyndon B. Johnson promises to win the "war on poverty"

Richard Nixon promises to quickly resolve the Vietnam War

George Bush Senior says "Read my lips: No new taxes"

Our country has accepted obligations that are difficult to fulfill, and would be dishonorable to abandon. Yet because we have acted in the great liberating tradition of this nation, tens of millions have achieved their freedom. And as hope kindles hope, millions more will find it. By our efforts, we have lit a fire as well—a fire in the minds of men. It warms those who feel its power, it burns those who fight its progress, and one day this untamed fire of freedom will reach the darkest corners of our world.

GEORGE W. BUSH, b. 1946, second inaugural address, 2005

First they ignore you, then they laugh at you, then they fight you, then you win.

MAHATMA GANDHI, 1869–1948

RELIGION

God is the perfect poet.

ROBERT BROWNING, 1812–1889, English poet

It is a fine thing to establish one's own religion in one's heart, not to be dependent on tradition and second-hand ideals. Life will seem to you, later, not a lesser, but a greater thing.

D. H. LAWRENCE, 1885–1930, English writer

A man can no more diminish God's glory by refusing to worship Him than a lunatic can put out the sun by scribbling the word, "darkness" on the walls of his cell.

C. S. LEWIS, 1898–1963, The Problem of Pain *(1940)*

Confucianism, the ancient Chinese religion, is often described as a creed of "optimistic humanism," grounded in a highly upbeat view of man's capabilities, teaching that human beings are perfectible through endeavor.

This most beautiful System of the Sun, Planets and Comets, could only proceed from the counsel and dominion of an intelligent and powerful being.

ISAAC NEWTON, 1642–1727, English scientist and philosopher,
Philosophiae Naturalis Principia Mathematica *(1687)*

True religion is real living; living with all one's soul, with all one's goodness and righteousness.

ALBERT EINSTEIN, 1879–1955, German-born physicist

The best remedy for those who are afraid, lonely or un-happy is to go outside, somewhere where they can be quiet, alone with the heavens, nature and God. Because only then does one feel that all is as it should be and that God wishes to see people happy, amidst the simple beauty of nature.

ANNE FRANK, 1929–1945

I cannot imagine how the clockwork of the universe can exist without a clockmaker.

VOLTAIRE, 1694–1778

This is my simple religion. There is no need for temples; no need for complicated philosophy. Our own brain, our own heart is our temple; the philosophy is kindness.

DALAI LAMA, b. 1935, Tibetan spiritual leader

According to research, those in the United States who believe in God give, on average, over 50 percent more to human-welfare charities than nonreligious people do.

SCIENCE

SCIENCE

. . . is simply commonsense at its best.
T. H. HUXLEY, 1825–1895, English biologist

. . . is the great antidote to the poison of enthusiasm and superstition.
ADAM SMITH, 1723–1790, Scottish philosopher

. . . is the poetry of reality.
RICHARD DAWKINS, b. 1941, English biologist

. . . knows no country, because knowledge belongs to humanity, and is the torch which illuminates the world.
LOUIS PASTEUR, 1822–1895, French chemist

One of the greatest gifts science has brought to the world is continuing elimination of the supernatural, and it was a lesson that my father passed on to me, that knowledge liberates mankind from superstition. We can live our lives without the constant fear that we have offended this or that deity who must be placated by incantation or sacrifice, or that we are at the mercy of devils or the Fates.
JAMES D. WATSON, b. 1928, co-discoverer of the structure of DNA,
Darwin, the Indelible Stamp: The Evolution of an Idea *(2005)*

Since the invention of the wheel some five thousand years ago, via proper sanitation and antibiotics, humans have consistently used their wit and skills to improve their lot. Below is the U.S. National Academy of Engineering's list of the top twenty greatest engineering achievements of the twentieth century:

1	Electrification	11	Highways
2	Automobile	12	Spacecraft
3	Airplane	13	Internet
4	Water supply and distribution	14	Imaging
5	Electronics	15	Household appliances
6	Radio and television	16	Health technologies
7	Agricultural mechanization	17	Petroleum and petrochemical technologies
8	Computers	18	Laser and fiber optics
9	Telephone	19	Nuclear technologies
10	Air conditioning and refrigeration	20	High-performance materials

The most beautiful thing we can experience is the mysterious. It is the source of all true art and science.
ALBERT EINSTEIN, 1879–1955, *German-born physicist*

In early 2008, the following fourteen challenges were laid down to scientists by the American Association for the Advancement of Science:

- Make solar energy affordable
- Provide energy from fusion
- Develop carbon sequestration
- Manage the nitrogen cycle
- Provide access to clean water
- Reverse engineer the brain
- Prevent nuclear terror
- Secure cyberspace
- Enhance virtual reality
- Improve urban infrastructure
- Advance health informatics
- Engineer better medicines
- Advance personalized learning
- Explore natural frontiers

In 2005, in celebration of its 125th anniversary, the world's largest science journal, *Science*, published 125 questions that are still a puzzle. The full list is at www.sciencemag.org/sciext/125th, and it includes such exciting and important conundrums as:

Are we alone in the universe? Is morality hardwired into the brain? Why do we sleep? What causes schizophrenia? What causes autism? What are human races, and how did they develop? How much can human life span be extended? What caused mass extinctions? What causes ice ages? What can replace cheap oil—and when?

SEX

When I glimpse the back of a woman's knees I seem to hear the first movement of Beethoven's Pastoral Symphony.

CHARLES GREVILLE, *1794–1865, British diarist*

It doesn't matter what you do in the bedroom as long as you don't do it in the street and frighten the horses.

MRS. PATRICK CAMPBELL, *1865–1940, English actress*

ANY WHICH WAY

In 1524, Renaissance author Pietro Aretino more-or-less invented Western pornography with his Sixteen Postures, sonnets written to accompany erotic drawings. (Casanova was to spend a New Year's Eve, almost exactly two hundred years later, trying Aretino's "Straight Tree" position out on a nun.) In the mid-twentieth century, Doctor Alfred C. Kinsey categorized six basic positions in his reports on human sexual behavior: man on top; woman on top; side by side; rear entrance; sitting; standing. But don't despair if you feel that this is too reductive; it has been estimated that there are at least four million possible sexual positions for a man and a woman.

Some of Those Four Million Sexual Positions:

The *Kama Sutra,* the ancient Hindu book of erotic love, describes sixty-four kinds of sexual acts, including *The Windmill, The Crab, Splitting the Bamboo, The Mare's Trap* and *The Lotus Seat,* and other examples from Arabic manuals and Chinese books on the Art of the Bedchamber include: *Cat and Mouse in the Same Hole; Old Man Pushing a Wheelbarrow; Phoenix Sporting in the Cinnabar Cleft; Congress of an Ass; The Donkeys of Late Spring; Fixing a Nail; Hovering Butterflies; Swinging Monkey; The Rooster Perches on a Stick; The Unicorn's Horn; The Toothpick in the Vulva.* Finally, one from Aristophanes' *Lysistrata* (411 BC) might make you reconsider the Missionary Position. It requires a woman to crouch with her buttocks in the air, and it's called *The Lioness on the Cheese Grater.*

Today's transgender movement is a roiling, radical critique of the limit of gender roles, with folks living in totally new categories, such as non-op transsexual, TG butch, femme queen, gender queer, cross-dresser, third gender, drag king or queen and transboy . . . all the aspects of sexual dimorphism are up for mix and match to suit our psychological needs and aesthetic preferences. By the twenty-second century, when we are facing indefinite life spans, tweaks to biological gender will become increasingly common, to stay in fashion, to improve your chances in life and love, or just out of curiosity.

JAMES HUGHES, executive director, Institute for Ethics and Emerging Technologies

Here is a small selection of **aphrodisiacs** which have all been hopefully promoted, with varying degrees of success, at some time or place:

- **Artichokes** (an old French street cry was "Artichokes! Artichokes! Heats the body and the spirit! Heats the genitals!")
- **Avocado** (hangs in pairs from the "testicle tree," and once considered so powerful that they were forbidden to virgins)
- **Chocolate** (packed with potent chemicals and used enthusiastically by the Aztecs)
- **Ginger** (made into a paste and rubbed on stomach, scrotum, and anus, according to Pliny the Elder, AD 23–79)
- **Pearls dissolved in vinegar** (a speciality of Cleopatra's)
- **Seafood** (mussels and crabs, according to the ancient Greeks; caviar; Casanova ate about fifty zinc-rich oysters a day)
- **Truffles** (fungi which give off chemicals similar to human sex hormones and praised by Rabelais, Napoleon, and Mme de Pompadour)
- **Vanilla** (from the Latin for vagina; sex psychologist Henry Havelock Ellis once visited a vanilla-processing factory and found that all the men had permanent erections)
- **Viagra** (cleared for sale by the FDA in 1998, as the first effective oral treatment for impotence. Even if it can provoke abnormal hair growth, burping and hiccups, it works)

AUTOMATIC RESPONSE

It was Woody Allen who pointed out that being bisexual doubles your chances of a date on a Saturday night; but soon your sex appeal—or lack of—will no longer be an issue. In 2006, Doctor Henrik Christensen, director of the Center for Robotics and Intelligent Machines at Georgia Tech, predicted that people will be having sex with robots by 2011.

Prostitutes for pleasure, concubines for services, wives for breeding and a melon for ecstasy.

Attributed to Sir Richard Burton, *1821–1890, English explorer*

SLEEP

In the Land of Nod at last.

Robert Louis Stevenson, *1850–1894, Scottish writer,* A Child's Garden of Verses *(1885)*

Blessings on him who invented sleep, the mantle that covers all human thoughts, the food that satisfies hunger, the drink that slakes thirst, the fire that warms cold, the cold that moderates heat, and, lastly, the common currency that buys all things, the balance and weight that equalizes the shepherd and the king, the simpleton and the sage.

Miguel de Cervantes, *1547–1616,* Don Quixote *(1605)*

While we are asleep in this world, we are awake in another one; in this way, every man is two men.
Attributed to JORGE LUIS BORGES, 1899–1986, quoted in John Russell's The Meaning of Modern Art *(1974)*

Sleep isn't just lying flat and being dead to the world. It is an active process, part light, part deep. When we enter REM, or Rapid Eye Movement sleep, scientists believe our bodies are undergoing an all-important repairing process for enhancing memories. Non-REM sleep is essential to restoring energy and concentration.

Whatever we may say, the happiest moment of the happy man is that of his falling asleep, just as the unhappiest moment of the unhappy man is that of his awakening.
ARTHUR SCHOPENHAUER, 1788–1860, German philosopher, The World as Will and Representation *(1844)*

Medical researchers have pinpointed some very clear steps to ensuring a good night's sleep: (1) clear your mind of stressful thoughts; (2) reduce alcohol consumption, caffeine, and meal sizes; (3) stick to a routine and go to bed at the same time; (4) cut out noise as much as possible, as well as excessive heat; (5) avoid medicines with stimulants; (6) do not watch TV or use a computer prior to sleep; (7) use thick curtains or shutters to block out early light. To maximize your chances of a good night, examine the feng-shui of your bedroom, too. It may be that objects like mirrors, computers, artificial lights, electric clocks, or the position of the bed are disrupting the harmony of the room.

Now I lay me down to sleep. I pray the Lord my soul to keep. Angels guard me through the night and wake me with the morning light.

Bedtime prayer

SMOKING

What a blessing this smoking is! Perhaps the greatest that we owe to the discovery of America.

Sir Arthur Helps, 1813–1875, British writer

The number of smokers is falling in developed nations. In the United States, smoking rates shrunk by nearly half from the mid-1960s to the mid-1990s, falling to 23 percent of adults by 1997 and 21 percent by 2007. Around 10 million adults smoke cigarettes in the UK today, roughly one sixth of the population. In 1974, just under half the adult population smoked. In the late 1940s nearly 70 percent of British grown-ups smoked cigarettes.

Men who had stopped smoking by the time they were thirty lived as long as those who never smoked, according to a fifty-year study involving 34,439 men published in the *British Medical Journal* in 2004. Those quitting at forty lived on average just one year less than those who had never smoked. Those who stopped smoking at fifty added six years onto their lives, while those who kicked the habit at sixty added an extra three years to their life.

Twentieth Century Tobacco Ads

Why risk sore throats? (Old Gold)

I light a Lucky and go light on the sweets. That's how I keep in shape and always look peppy. To stay slender reach for a Lucky! A most effective way of retaining a trim figure. (Lucky Strike)

Smoke as many as you want. They never get on your nerves. (Camel)

Lastly (and this is, perhaps, the golden rule) no woman should marry a teetotaller, or a man who does not smoke.

ROBERT LOUIS STEVENSON, *1850–1894,* Virginibus Puerisque *(1881)*

According to a recent nationwide survey: MORE DOCTORS SMOKE CAMELS THAN ANY OTHER CIGARETTE! Family physicians, surgeons, diagnosticians, nose and throat specialists, doctors in every branch of medicine . . . a total of 113,597 doctors were asked the question: What cigarette do you smoke? And more of them named Camel as their smoke than any other cigarette!

American advertisement from the 1950s

He who lives without tobacco is not worthy to live.
MOLIÈRE, 1622–1673, French playwright, Don Juan

Those who smoke outnumber those who do not by a hundred to one . . . so non-smokers must learn to adapt themselves to existing conditions . . . and when they come into contact with smokers, it is scarcely fair that the few should be allowed to prohibit the many from the pursuit of their comforts and their pleasures.
Good Housekeeping, *1940*

TRAVEL

Make voyages!—Attempt them! There's nothing else.
TENNESSEE WILLIAMS, 1911–1983, Camino Real *(1953)*

According to Psychology Professor Frank Drews, at the University of Utah, about 80 percent of drivers think they're better at driving than the average motorist!

At the moment, flying only accounts for 2 percent of the world's carbon emissions but, with the aviation industry expanding at 5 percent a year, airplanes need to clean up their act. Researchers are looking at four ways of doing this:

1 Make the planes of lightweight materials as strong as metal but as light as plastic, thereby cutting fuel use dramatically.
2 Replace turbojet engines with much lighter, contra-rotating fans.
3 Rationalize international air-traffic control, so that planes fly from A to B rather than dithering around blasting out fuel.
4 Discover and use environmentally friendly fuel—which is still the Holy Grail: one idea, which is a far-off but apparently realistic prospect, is to fit micro-organisms with artificial chromosomes, so that they can convert sunshine into fuel; hydrogen-powered aircraft are also a possibility.

DUBLIN, AUGUST 25, 1990

When asked what he would do after four and a half years' captivity in Beirut, Brian Keenan replied: "I'm going to visit all the countries in the world, eat all the food in the world, drink all the drink and make love, I hope, to all the women in the world, and maybe then get a good night's sleep."

In 2007, the British Interplanetary Society hosted a conference of physicists entitled *Faster than Light: Breaking the Interstellar Distance Barrier*. While there's little chance of any of us traveling at warp speed in the very near future, it's reckoned that humankind is on the way to learning the secret of warp speed, which would involve bending the very fabric of space and time in order to travel faster than the speed of light. To infinity and beyond . . . !

For my part, I travel not to go anywhere, but to go. I travel for travel's sake. The great affair is to move; to feel the needs and hitches of our life more nearly; to come down off this feather-bed of civilisation, and find the globe granite underfoot and strewn with cutting flints.

ROBERT LOUIS STEVENSON, *1850–1894*

The world is a book, and those who do not travel, read only a page.

ST. AUGUSTINE, *354–430*, City of God

TRUTH

I'm for truth, no matter who tells it. I'm for justice, no matter who it's for or against.

MALCOLM X, *1925–1965, civil rights activist*

Truth is tough. It will not break, like a bubble, at a touch; nay, you may kick it about all day like a football, and it will be round and full at evening.

OLIVER WENDELL HOLMES, *1809–1894, American author*

Three things cannot long be hidden: the sun, the moon, and the truth.

CONFUCIUS, *551–471 BC*

For who knows not that Truth is strong next to the Almighty? She needs no policies, no stratagems, nor licensings to make her victorious.

JOHN MILTON, 1608–1674, Areopagitica: A Speech for the Liberty of Unlicensed Printing (1644)

I maintain that Truth is a pathless land, and you cannot approach it by any path whatsoever, by any religion, by any sect.

J. KRISHNAMURTI, 1895–1986, Indian writer and speaker, during a speech in Holland, August 3, 1929

Truth exists; only lies are invented.

GEORGES BRAQUE, 1882–1963, French painter and sculptor

The truth cannot be contained in one single dream.

Arab proverb

When will women begin to have the first glimmer that above all other loyalties is the loyalty to Truth, i.e., to yourself, that husband, children, friends and country are as nothing to that.

ALICE JAMES, 1848–1892, diary entry November 19, 1889

Truth is the glue that holds governments together. Compromise is the oil that makes governments go.

GERALD FORD, 1913–2006, U.S. president

I believe that unarmed truth and unconditional love will have the final word in reality. This is why right, temporarily defeated, is stronger than evil triumphant.

MARTIN LUTHER KING JR., 1929–1968, civil rights activist

UNITED STATES

America is the greatest, freest and most decent society in existence. It is an oasis of goodness in a desert of cynicism and barbarism. This country, once an experiment unique in the world, is now the last best hope for the world.

DINESH D'SOUZA, b. 1961, Indian-born American author

I always consider the settlement of America with reverence and wonder, as the opening of a grand scene and design in providence, for the illumination of the ignorant and the emancipation of the slavish part of mankind all over the earth.

JOHN ADAMS, 1735–1826, second U.S. president

We must be the great arsenal of democracy.

FRANKLIN D. ROOSEVELT, 1882–1945, U.S. president

Citizens of the United States have been awarded a total of 304 Nobel prizes, almost three times more than Britain, the second most decorated country. There have been twenty peace prize winners including Al Gore (2007), Jimmy Carter (2002), Martin Luther King Jr. (1964), George C. Marshall (1953), the Quakers (1947), Frank B. Kellogg (1929), Woodrow Wilson (1919), and Theodore Roosevelt (1906).

You cannot spill a drop of American blood without spilling the blood of the whole world . . . We are not a nation, so much as a world.

HERMAN MELVILLE, 1819–1891, American novelist

Sometimes people call me an idealist. Well, that is the way I know I am an American. America is the only idealistic nation in the world.

WOODROW WILSON, 1856–1924, U.S. president

For we must consider that we shall be as a city upon a hill. The eyes of all people are upon us. So that if we shall deal falsely with our God in this work we have undertaken . . . we shall be made a story and a by-word throughout the world. We shall open the mouths of enemies to speak evil of the ways of God . . . We shall shame the faces of many of God's worthy servants, and cause their prayers to be turned into curses upon us til we be consumed out of the good land whither we are a-going,

JOHN WINTHROP, 1588–1649, warning to Puritan settlers of New England in 1630

The American, by nature, is optimistic. He is experimental, an inventor and a builder who builds best when called upon to build greatly.

JOHN F. KENNEDY, 1917–1963, U.S. president

There is nothing wrong with America that cannot be cured by what is right with America.

BILL CLINTON, b. 1946, U.S. president, first inaugural address in 1993

WAR

The war in Vietnam is going well and will succeed.
ROBERT MCNAMARA, b. 1916, U.S. secretary of defense,
January 1963

And for myself, I have done my duty. I have identified my fate with that of the heroic dead, & whatever lies these sordid exploiters of human misery spread about us these officials, there is a right & a God to fight for and our fight has been worth fighting. I do not despair—nor complain—It has been a great cause.
FLORENCE NIGHTINGALE, 1820–1910, in a letter to sister
Parthenope from Scutari, Crimea

I just want you to know that, when we talk about war, we're really talking about peace.
GEORGE W. BUSH, b. 1946, U.S. president

A professional soldier understands that war means killing people, war means maiming people, war means families left without fathers and mothers. All you have to do is hold your first dying soldier in your arms, and have that terribly futile feeling that his life is flowing out and you can't do anything about it. Then you understand the horror of war. Any soldier worth his salt should be antiwar. And still, there are things worth fighting for.
GENERAL NORMAN SCHWARZKOPF, b. 1934

You will be home before the leaves have fallen from the trees.

KAISER WILHELM II, 1859–1941, to the German troops, August 1914

With these now infamous words, under a floating banner proclaiming "**Mission Accomplished**," President George W. Bush stood on the deck of a U.S. battleship, in May 2003, and declared the Iraq war over: "Admiral Kelly, Captain Card, officers and sailors of the U.S.S. *Abraham Lincoln*, my fellow Americans: Major combat operations in Iraq have ended. In the Battle of Iraq, the United States and our allies have prevailed. And now our coalition is engaged in securing and reconstructing that country."

While war is terribly destructive, monstrously cruel, and horrible beyond expressions, it nevertheless causes the divine spark in men to glow, to kindle, and to burst into a living flame, and enables them to attain heights of devotion to duty, sheer heroism, and sublime unselfishness that in all probability they would never have reached in the prosecution of peaceful pursuits.

MAJOR-GENERAL JOHN A. LEJEUNE, 1867–1942, Reminiscences of a Marine *(1929)*

Whatever happens, the U.S. Navy is not going to be caught napping.

FRANK KNOX, 1874–1944, U.S. secretary of the Navy, on December 4, 1941, three days before the attack on Pearl Harbor

There is no immediate prospect of an invasion.

GERD VON RUNDSTEDT, 1875–1953, German field marshal, on the evening of June 5, 1945 to German forces he commanded in France

WEALTH

Ten Richest People in the World
(in billions of dollars)

Warren Buffett (U.S., stocks): 62

Carlos Slim (Mexico, telecommunications): 60

Bill Gates (U.S., software): 58

Lakshmi Mittal (India, steel): 45

Mukesh Ambani (India, various): 43

Anil Ambani (India, various): 42

Ingvar Kamprad (Sweden, flat pack furniture): 31

K. P. Singh (U.S., property): 30

Oleg Deripaska (Russia, natural resources): 28

Karl Albrecht (Germany, supermarkets): 27

Source: Forbes 2008

"Gross National Happiness" is a concept created by the **King of Bhutan His Majesty Jigme Singye Wangchuck** in 1972 as an alternative measure for gauging the development and state of countries. Rooted in the Buddhist idea that inner peace and happiness is more important than material wealth, GNH encourages people to look beyond dry economic measurements such as GNP to assess the value of our lives. In Britain, the New Economics Foundation has developed its own audit of success, the Happy Planet Index, which also includes environmental factors. Go to www.neweconomics.org for more information.

We believe that once the peoples including their corporations and labor and other organizations of the world, understand the benefits of a single global currency, they will demand it from their governments. The single global currency is what the peoples of the world need, and it is what they want.

Single Global Currency Association

Ten Richest Countries by GNP per capita

Luxembourg $56,380   Iceland $37,920
Norway $51,810   Japan $37,050
Switzerland $49,600   Sweden $35,840
United States $41,440   Ireland $34,310
Denmark $40,750   United Kingdom $33,630
(World Bank 2006)

Britain became the largest donor to the World Bank's main fund for assistance to poor countries when it overtook the United States in 2007. The total of $25.1 billion pledged by the world's richest countries was a record sum, up 41 percent from the bank's previous raising campaign in 2005. The sum included donations by China and Egypt, countries that were once recipients of such aid.

Eight of the ten most severe stock market crashes happened in the early part of the twentieth century, indicating that either economies have developed better self-defense mechanisms or that governments have learned to manage economies better.

World's Most Generous Philanthropists in 2007 and Their Donations in Millions

Warren Buffett, $40,650

Bill and Melinda Gates, $3,519

George Kaiser, $2,271

George Soros, $2,109

Gordon and Betty Moore, $2,067

Walton (Wal-Mart) family, $1,475

Herbert and Marion Sandler, $1,368

Eli and Edythe Broad, $1,216

Donald Bren, $915

Jon Huntsman, $800

(*Source:* Forbes)

WOMEN

The surest remedy for the male disease of self-contempt is the love of a sensible woman.

FRIEDRICH NIETZSCHE, Human, All-Too-Human *(1878)*

Woman seems to differ from man in mental disposition, chiefly in her greater tenderness and less selfishness . . .

CHARLES DARWIN, The Descent of Man *(1871)*

The Weaker Sex?

According to Thomas Perls of the Boston University School of Medicine, women, evolutionarily speaking, are more fit than men—evolution naturally selects the genes of women who live long and age slowly (because they can bear and raise more children) over those who die young. Women outlive men in all developed and most undeveloped countries, sometimes by as much as ten years, and they've been outsurviving men since at least the 1500s, in spite of the sizable risk of childbirth. Remarkably, this gender gap is most pronounced in the really old: among centenarians worldwide, women outnumber men *nine to one.*

Women are the real architects of society.
Harriet Beecher Stowe, 1811–1896, American author

The cocks may crow, but it's the hen that lays the egg.
Margaret Thatcher, b. 1925, British prime minister

We have to free half of the human race, the women, so that they can help to free the other half.
Emmeline Pankhurst, 1858–1928, suffragist

We are not asking for superiority for we have always had that; all we ask is equality.
Nancy Astor, 1879–1964, first female member of the British parliament

---

March 8th is International Women's Day (www.un.org/events/women/iwd), but it is also the day when the Global Women's Strike is held each year to highlight just how much of the world's work is done by women, and the difference it makes when their contribution is withdrawn. Other issues pointed out on the website at www.globalwomenstrike.net include the fact that a mere 10 percent of the world's annual $1 trillion military budget would provide everyone in the world with basic health care, enough food and drinkable water, proper sanitation, literacy, and a minimum income.

Sure, Fred Astaire was great, but don't forget that Ginger Rogers did everything he did, backwards . . . and in high heels.

Bob Thaves, 1924–2006, American cartoonist, in Frank and Ernest

Some 2,500 years ago, the great Greek playwright Aristophanes wrote *Lysistrata*, the story of a woman who, during the Peloponnesian War, persuades her fellow wives to go on a sex strike in order to force their husbands to vote for peace with Sparta. Her reasoning is as follows:

> We need only sit indoors with painted cheeks, and meet our mates lightly clad in transparent gowns of Amorgos silk, and perfectly depilated; they will get their tools up and be wild to lie with us. That will be the time to refuse, and they will hasten to make peace, I am convinced of that.

In real life, sex strikes have been used by women: in Sudan, to protest against the civil war; in Colombia to protest against drug wars; in Poland to fight for legal abortion; and in Turkey to fight for the rights of communities against poisonous cyanide-based gold mining.

What the woman who labors wants is the right to live, not simply exist—the right to life as the rich woman has it; the right to life, and the sun, and music, and art . . . The worker must have bread, but she must have roses, too.

ROSE SCHNEIDERMAN, *1882–1972, American socialist*

WORK

There is no success without hard work.
SOPHOCLES, c. 496–405 BC, Electra

Work banishes those three great evils, boredom, vice, and poverty.
VOLTAIRE, 1694–1778, Candide

Most people questioned in opinion polls on job satisfaction give **"respect from their boss"** as the biggest source of work happiness.

Work pays for debts. Laziness creates them.
French proverb

Work earnestly at anything, you will by degrees learn to work at all things.
THOMAS CARLYLE, 1795–1881, Past and Present *(1843)*

Work is the true elixir of life. The busiest man is the happiest man. Excellence in any art or profession is attained only by hard and persistent work.
GEORGE ORWELL, 1903–1950, English journalist and novelist

Far and away the best prize that life has to offer is the chance to work hard at work worth doing.
THEODORE ROOSEVELT, 1858–1919, U.S. president

In every rank, or great or small, 'Tis industry supports us all.

JOHN GAY, 1685–1732, "Man, Cat, Dog, and Fly"

I like work; it fascinates me. I can sit and look at it for hours. I love to keep it by me: the idea of getting rid of it nearly breaks my heart.

JEROME K. JEROME, 1859–1927, Three Men in a Boat (1889)

YOUTH

A ten-year longevity study from America has shown that having lots of children, four ideally, can increase your chances of longevity, especially in men.

If help and salvation are to come, they can only come from the children, for the children are the makers of men.

MARIA MONTESSORI, 1870–1952, Italian educator

Children have neither past nor future. They live in the present, something which rarely happens to us.

JEAN DE LA BRUYERE, 1645–1696, Les Caracteres ou les moeurs de ce siecle, De l'Homme (1688)

Adolescence is the only time when we can learn something.

MARCEL PROUST, *1871–1922*, À la recherche du temps perdu *(1919)*

If you want to be creative, stay in part a child, with the creativity and invention that characterizes children before they are deformed by adult society.

JEAN PIAGET, *1896–1980, Swiss philosopher*

The child shall have the right to freedom of expression; this right shall include freedom to seek, receive and impart information and ideas of all kinds, regardless of frontiers, either orally, in writing or in print, in the form of art, or through any other media of the child's choice.

Article 13.1 Convention of the Rights of the Child (1989)

Let our children grow tall, and some taller than others if they have it in them to do so.

MARGARET THATCHER, *b. 1925, from a speech in October 1975*

And they brought unto him also infants, that he would touch them: but when his disciples saw it, they rebuked them. But Jesus called them unto him, and said, Suffer little children to come unto me, and forbid them not: for of such is the kingdom of God. Verily I say unto you, Whosoever shall not receive the kingdom of God as a little child shall in no wise enter therein.

Luke 18: 15–17

One generation plants the trees; another gets the shade.
Chinese proverb

Love children especially, for like the angels they too are sinless, and they live to soften and purify our hearts, and, as it were, to guide us. Woe to him who offends a child!
FYODOR DOSTOYEVSKY, *1821–1881, Russian writer,*
The Brothers Karamazov (*1880*)

The Pessimist's Handbook

The
PESSIMIST'S
Handbook

A Companion to
DESPAIR

NIALL EDWORTHY
& PETRA CRAMSIE

Free Press
New York London Toronto Sydney

*f*P Free Press
A Division of Simon & Schuster, Inc.
1230 Avenue of the Americas
New York, NY 10020

Copyright © 2008 by Niall Edworthy and Petra Cramsie
Published simultaneously in Great Britain by Transworld Publishers
Illustrations by Emily Faccini
Half-title illustrations copyright © 2008 by Ray Fenwick

Page 3: Lines from "Advice to Young Women" from *Serious Concerns* by Wendy Cope ©
Wendy Cope 2006. Page 3: Logan Pearsall Smith quoted by kind permission of the London
Library. Page 5: Susan Ertz, *Anger in the Sky*, Hodder & Stoughton 1943. Page 5: Reproduced
from an article in the Sunday Times by John Mortimer, Oct. 5, 2003 (Copyright © John
Mortimer 2003) by permission of PFD (www.pfd.co.uk) on behalf of John Mortimer. Page
7: Reproduced from a quotation by Evelyn Waugh (source unknown) Copyright © Estate
of Evelyn Waugh by permission of PFD (www.pfd.co.uk) on behalf of the Estate of Evelyn
Waugh. Page 23: From *A Writer's Notebook* by W. Somerset Maugham, published by Secker &
Warburg. Reprinted by permission of The Random House Group Ltd. Page 24: Stevie Smith
quoted with kind permission of the Estate of James MacGibbon. Page 45: J.G. Ballard,
Interview with Andrea Juno and V. Vale *Re/Search*, No. 8/9 (1984). Page 53: Fran Lebowitz,
Metropolitan Life, 1978, published by Sidgwick & Jackson. Page 60: *Shooting an Elephant and Other
Essays* by George Orwell (Copyright © George Orwell, 1946). Page 77: Quotation from *The
Future of an Illusion* by Sigmund Freud reproduced by arrangement with Paterson Marsh Ltd,
London. Page 83: Reproduced with permission of Curtis Brown Group Ltd, London, on
behalf of David Lodge. Copyright © David Lodge 1965. Page 102: Copyright © 2008 by Al
Gore, reprinted with permission of the Wylie Agency, Inc. Page 108: "Unfortunate Coinci-
dence," copyright 1926, renewed © 1954 by Dorothy Parker, from *The Portable Dorothy Parker*
by Dorothy Parker, edited by Marion Meade. Used by permission of Viking Penguin, a division of Penguin Group (USA) Inc. Page 115: Joseph Alois Schumpeter, 1883–1950, *Capitalism,
Socialism and Democracy*, Ch. 14. Routledge, 1942. By permission of Harvard University.

First Free Press trade paperback edition November 2009

FREE PRESS and colophon are trademarks of Simon & Schuster, Inc.

For information about special discounts for bulk purchases, please contact Simon & Schuster
Special Sales at 1-866-456-6798 or at business@simonandschuster.com.

The Simon & Schuster Speakers Bureau can bring authors to your live event. For more information or to book an event contact the Simon & Schuster Speakers Bureau at 1-866-248-3049 or
visit our website at www.simonspeakers.com.

Designed by Ellen R. Sasahara

Manufactured in the United States of America

10 9 8 7 6 5 4 3 2 1

Library of Congress Cataloging-in-Publication Data
Edworthy, Niall.
    The optimist's handbook : a companion to hope / Niall Edworthy and Petra Cramsie.
        p. cm.
    Title on added title page: Pessimist's handbook : a companion to despair
1. Conduct of life—Humor. 2. Conduct of life—Quotations, maxims, etc. I. Cramsie, Petra.
II. Title. III. Title: Pessimist's handbook : a companion to despair.
    PN6231.C6142E39   2008
    082—dc22   041262

ISBN 978-1-4391-0166-7
ISBN 978-1-4391-5953-8 (pbk)

CATEGORIES

ADVENTURE

Fools rush in where angels fear to tread.
ALEXANDER POPE, 1688–1744, English poet

A life without adventure is likely to be unsatisfying, but a life in which adventure is allowed to take whatever form it will is sure to be short.
BERTRAND RUSSELL, 1872–1970, British philosopher

Had we lived I should have had a tale to tell of the hardihood, endurance and courage of my companions which would have stirred the heart of every Englishman. These rough notes and our dead bodies must tell the tale.
CAPTAIN ROBERT FALCON SCOTT's last message to the world, March 25, 1912

So many centuries after the Creation it is unlikely that anyone could find hitherto unknown lands of any value.
Committee advising Ferdinand and Isabella regarding Columbus's proposal for a journey of discovery (1486)

Caution is the eldest child of wisdom.
VICTOR HUGO, 1802–1885, French poet

It is better to be careful a hundred times than to be killed once.
Proverb

At the end of January 2008 Englishman Mark Boyle set out from his hometown of Bristol on a two-and-a-half-year, 9,000-mile pilgrimage to the birthplace of Mahatma Gandhi to highlight the kindness of his fellow man. The plan was to get to India without spending any money and by surviving on the kindness of people he met along the way, as a protest against commercialism. He got as far as Calais. "People seemed to think I was some kind of refugee," said the crestfallen adventurer, explaining the language problems that derailed his journey in optimism. "They thought I was begging." Boyle conceded his idiosyncratic appearance may also have been a factor in his failure to prise more than a chocolate bar and a small bag of nuts from his French cousins. Commenting on his electric yellow trousers, open sandals, and blackened toe nails, the organic food store manager added: "In France, clearly they are a bit more sophisticated and they weren't impressed."

I love the angelic in his figure, which reminds me of Shelley: the peculiarly and very mysteriously veiled, unapproachable, withdrawing, unadventurous flavour of his being, that not wanting to know, that rejection of material experience, the sublime incest of his fantastically delicate and seductive art.

THOMAS MANN, *1875–1955, German writer, on composer Frédéric Chopin in* Doctor Faustus *(1947)*

Adventure is just bad planning.

ROALD AMUNDSEN, *1872–1928, Norwegian explorer*

ADVICE

Advice is seldom welcome; and those who want it the most always like it the least.
LORD CHESTERFIELD, 1694–1773, Letters to His Son

Believe everything you hear about the world; nothing is too impossibly bad.
HONORÉ DE BALZAC, 1799–1850, novelist and playwright

There's no need to worry—
Whatever you do, life is hell.
WENDY COPE, b. 1945, poet, "Advice to Young Women"

Live with yourself: get to know how poorly furnished you are.
PERSIUS, 34–62 AD, Satires

Cheer up! The worst is yet to come!
PHILANDER CHASE JOHNSON, 1866–1939, journalist, in Everybody's Magazine, *1920*

How many of our daydreams would darken into nightmares if there seemed any danger of their coming true!
LOGAN PEARSALL SMITH, 1865–1946, Afterthoughts *(1931)*

If we see light at the end of the tunnel,
It's the light of the oncoming train.
ROBERT LOWELL, 1917–1977, poet, "Day by Day"

A man must swallow a toad every morning if he wishes to be sure of finding nothing still more disgusting before the end of the day.
SÉBASTIEN-ROCH NICOLAS DE CHAMFORT, 1741–1794

Love thy neighbour, but don't take down the fence.
BENJAMIN FRANKLIN, 1706–1790

My only solution for the problem of habitual accidents (and, so far, nobody has asked me for my solution) is to stay in bed all day. Even then, there is always the chance that you will fall out.
ROBERT BENCHLEY, 1889–1945, "Safety Second," Chips off the Old Benchley *(1949)*

Do not bite at the bait of pleasure till you know there is no hook beneath it.

Thomas Jefferson, 1743–1826

AFTERLIFE

The eternal silence of these infinite spaces (the heavens) terrifies me.

Blaise Pascal, 1623–1662, mathematician, Pensées

Millions long for immortality who don't know what to do with themselves on a rainy Sunday afternoon.

Susan Ertz, 1894–1985, American novelist, Anger in the Sky

Hell is an all-male black-tie dinner of chartered accountants which goes on for eternity.

John Mortimer, b. 1923, English barrister and writer, in The Sunday Times *(2003)*

The terrible meditation of hell fire and eternal punishment much torments a sinful silly soul. What's a thousand year to eternity? . . . a finger burnt by chance we may not endure, the pain is so grievous, we may not abide an hour, a night is intolerable; and what shall this unspeakable fire then be that burns for ever, innumerable infinite millions of years . . . O eternity!

Robert Burton, 1577–1640, English scholar, The Anatomy of Melancholy

The website www.near-death.com gathers together stories of people who have been through near-death experiences. Many were declared clinically dead before coming back to life, and some have been so deeply affected by their horrific visions of the Afterlife that they have never fully recovered. Bryan Melvin, who "died" in Arizona in 1980, recalls leaving his body and seeing a figure resembling Jesus, before being sucked toward a place of foul smells where dreadful creatures were held captive in small gelatinous and mirrored cubes. Tony Lawrence, senior lecturer in psychology at the University of Coventry, is currently studying negative near-death experiences, intrigued as to why people from such different backgrounds and religious beliefs, and with no particular profile for vice or drug taking, seem to share similarly terrifying visions of hell and eternal darkness.

A dungeon horrible, on all sides round
As one great furnace flamed, yet from those flames
No light, but rather darkness visible
Served only to discover sights of woe,
Regions of sorrow, doleful shades, where peace
And rest can never dwell, hope never comes
That comes to all; but torture without end
Still urges, and a fiery deluge, fed
With ever-burning sulphur unconsumed . . .
JOHN MILTON, *1608–1674, English poet, prose polemicist, and civil servant,* Paradise Lost

Ah well, there is just this world and then the next, and then all our troubles will be over with.

OLD LADY, QUOTED BY L. O. ASQUITH, *1864–1945, society wit*

It's a curious thing that every creed promises a paradise which will be absolutely uninhabitable for anyone of civilised taste.

EVELYN WAUGH, *1903–1966, English writer*

We have no reliable guarantee that the afterlife will be any less exasperating than this one, have we?

NOEL COWARD, *1899–1973,* Blithe Spirit

ALCOHOL

A drink that tasted, she thought, like weak vinegar mixed with a packet of pins.

H. G. WELLS, *1866–1946, on champagne,* Joan and Peter *(1918)*

The demon of intemperance ever seems to have delighted in sucking the blood of genius and generosity.

ABRAHAM LINCOLN, *1809–1865, U.S. president*

Wine hath drowned more men than the sea.

THOMAS FULLER, *1608–1661, English writer and physician*

A man who exposes himself when he is intoxicated, has not the art of getting drunk.

SAMUEL JOHNSON, *1709–1784, English writer*

Harris, I am not well, pray get me a glass of brandy. These were the words of the Prince of Wales (later George IV) on first seeing his future wife, Caroline of Brunswick, in 1795. The prince was so appalled by Caroline, whom he thought unattractive and unhygienic, that he went on a three-day drinking binge and had to be held up by his groomsmen at the wedding ceremony. The prince's letters show that the couple had sexual intercourse on three occasions, including twice on the first night, after which the future king, still stupefied with drink, slept in the bedroom fireplace. The third occasion took place the following night: Princess Charlotte, George's only legitimate child, was born from one of those presumably awkward unions on January 7, 1796, after which the couple began to live separate lives and were never seen together in public again.

Famous Alcoholics

Josef Stalin	Douglas Fairbanks
Bonnie Prince Charlie	Errol Flynn
Richard Burton	Judy Garland
Edgar Allen Poe	W. C. Fields
Ulysses S. Grant	Calamity Jane
Jackson Pollock	Hitler's father
Edward VIII	Boris Yeltsin

Drunkenness is nothing but voluntary madness.
SENECA, Roman philosopher

Drunkenness is temporary suicide.
BERTRAND RUSSELL, 1872–1970, British philosopher

ANIMALS

I confess freely to you, I never could look long upon a monkey, without very mortifying reflections.
WILLIAM CONGREVE, 1670–1729, English playwright and poet

I loathe people who keep dogs. They're cowards who have not got the guts to bite people themselves.
AUGUST STRINDBERG, 1849–1912, Swedish dramatist

That indefatigable and unsavoury engine of pollution, the dog.
JOHN SPARROW, 1906–1992, letter to The Times *(1975)*

Cat, n. A soft, indestructible automaton provided by nature to be kicked when things go wrong in the domestic circle.
AMBROSE BIERCE, 1842–c.1914, The Devil's Dictionary *(1911)*

A man who carries a cat by the tail learns something he can learn in no other way.
MARK TWAIN, 1835–1910, American humorist

Living Species

The irreversible loss of species, which by 2100 may reach one third of all species now living, is especially serious. We are losing the potential they hold for providing medicinal and other benefits, and the contribution that genetic diversity of life forms gives to the robustness of the world's biological systems and to the astonishing beauty of the earth itself. Much of this damage is irreversible on a scale of centuries or permanent. . . . Our massive tampering with the world's interdependent web of life—coupled with the environmental damage inflicted by deforestation, species loss, and climate change—could trigger widespread adverse effects, including unpredictable collapses of critical biological systems whose interactions and dynamics we only imperfectly understand.

The Holocene Extinction Event—that is, the first man-made mass extinction, is now well under way, with the rate of extinctions estimated at 100 to 1,000 times the usual, natural extinction rate. One terrible story, the life and death of the passenger pigeon, highlights mankind's wretched short-sightedness. Once the most common bird in North America, this pigeon would migrate in stupendously enormous flocks of about a billion birds—a mile wide and three hundred miles long—taking several days to pass. This proved such a temptation to the men with guns that, by the 1870s, the species was declining catastrophically. Martha, the last pathetic survivor out of five billion, died on September 1, 1914, in Cincinnati, Ohio.

Colony Collapse Disorder

In 2007, in the United States, 25 percent of the honey-bees in commercial hives simply disappeared. No dead bodies were found, just hives, mysteriously empty. In fact, in an unprecedented die-off, bee populations are starting to collapse worldwide and we don't know why. Is it because of genetically modified crops, pesticides, radiation from mobile phone networks, climate change, or something else? It's not just our honey that's in danger; a third of the world's food supply—an estimated 130,000 plants, from apples to zucchini—needs bees for pollination, while another third is indirectly supported by the hive of industry (cows need hay, hay needs bees). The workers from just one hive can visit a million flowers in a day. Who will do this if they disappear forever? Will the sound of a lazy summer's day in the future be not the hum of bees but the roar of giant blowers as desperate farmers attempt to pollinate their own crops?

ART & ARTISTS

What do these so-called artists mean when they preach the discovery of the "new"? Is there anything new? Everything has been done, everything has been discovered.
INGRES, 1780–1867, French painter, quoted in 1821 from Henri Delaborde, Ingres: sa vie, ses travaux, sa doctrine *(1870)*

Painting: The art of protecting flat surfaces from the weather and exposing them to the critic.
AMBROSE BIERCE, 1842–c.1914, The Devil's Dictionary *(1911)*

I thought it would be my one and only exhibition, so I decided to call it My Major Retrospective.
TRACEY EMIN, b. 1963, British artist

Sculpture is the art of the hole and the lump.
AUGUST RODIN, 1840–1917, French artist

Vincent van Gogh, who committed suicide after spending much of his life in abject poverty, having sold only one painting in his lifetime (to his brother) must be turning in his grave with the money he brings in now. In 1987, his Sunflowers sold for a world record price of $49 million—but nearly one hundred years too late for the artist.

Look, it's my misery that I have to paint this kind of painting, it's your misery that you have to love it, and the price of the misery is thirteen hundred and fifty dollars.
MARK ROTHKO, 1903–1970, American abstract expressionist

For all their labeling of much of modern art as degenerate, and their persecution of well-known artists such as Otto Dix and Oskar Kokoschka, the Nazis were also keen on plundering Old Masters. Over the course of World War II, everything from disused mines to museum vaults were used to stock hundreds of thousands of looted works of art, many stolen from murdered Jewish collectors. www.lostart.de is a database set up by the German government to register and trace lost artworks.

The canvas was always saying no to me.
ROMARE BEARDEN, 1914–1988, American painter

Every time I paint a portrait I lose a friend.
JOHN SINGER SARGENT, 1856–1925, American painter

BALDNESS

Good to see a lot of bald men here tonight. Did you first notice it, sir, when it took longer and longer to wash your face?
HARRY HILL, b. 1964, English stand-up comedian

One method of hiding hair loss is the "comb-over," which involves restyling the surviving hair in a literally vain attempt to cover the balding area. One word of advice, though: *don't.*

Bad News All Round

The greater the hair loss on the top of a man's head, the higher the risk of his having heart problems, according to research. Those with a receding hairline should not worry unduly, but those going bald at the crown should watch their lifestyle—yet not worry unduly either, since excessive worry can make your hair fall out.

If you must go out for a walk in the countryside, make sure you go bewigged or behatted—or risk suffering the fate of Aeschylus. On a sunny day in 456 BC, according to legend, the bald-pated playwright went for an innocent stroll in Sicily. A great eagle-like vulture, the Lammergeier, mistook his shiny head for a rock, and dropped a tortoise on it to smash it—(the tortoise, that is). In the event, Aeschylus's head was broken open; the tortoise got away with minor injuries.

An estimated two billion dollars is spent
in the United States every year, in the fight against
male pattern hair loss.

A man is usually bald four or five years before he knows it.
EDGAR WATSON HOWE, 1853–1937, American novelist

An Egyptian papyrus scroll dating back to at least 1,000 BC prescribes a crocodile-fat-and-hippopotamus-dung ointment for hair loss, which may be the reason that the pharaohs were never seen out in public without wigs on. Meanwhile, Hippocrates, the Father of Medicine, and not known for being a quack, recommended an application of cumin, pigeon droppings, nettles, and horseradish.

BEAUTY

A beautiful face is a dumb commendation.
PUBLILIUS SYRUS, first century BC, Latin writer

What is beauty, but a well-dressed skull that loses colour with the slightest illness, and, before death robs it of everything, the grace of its external and apparent surface is mortified by the years in such a way that, if eyes could penetrate within beauty, they could watch it only full of horror?
ANTONIO VIEIRA, 1608–1697, Portuguese missionary, Sermon of the Silent Devil *(1666)*

Beauty is but a flower
Which wrinkles will devour.
THOMAS NASHE, 1567–1601, Litany in Time of Plague *(1592)*

Piobbico is a small town in the Le Marche region of Italy and it is home to Italy's one and only *Club dei Brutti* (Ugly Club). Every year, on the first Sunday of September, the small town is thronging with ugly people who have come to celebrate the annual festival of ugliness. There is a top prize, and it has been awarded to a certain Telesforo Iacobelli for several years now.

No woman can be a beauty without a fortune.
GEORGE FARQUHAR, *1677–1707,* The Beaux Stratagem *(1707)*

BEAUTY IS IN THE EYE OF THE BEER HOLDER

BEAUTY IS ONLY SKIN DEEP.
UGLY GOES STRAIGHT TO THE BONE.

American bumper stickers

Gurning is the high art of pulling extremely ugly and completely repellent grimaces. It is generally done by sucking in one's cheeks, twisting the lips and popping out one's eyes as much as possible without causing damage to the face. Cumbria has been holding an annual gurning fair since 1267!

BOOKS

With a goose quill and a few sheets of paper I mock the universe.
PIETRO ARETINO, *1492–1557, Italian author*

The more books one reads, the more stupid one becomes.
MAO TSE-TUNG, *1893–1976, Chinese communist leader*

And what is the use of a book, thought Alice, without pictures or conversations?
LEWIS CARROLL, *1832–1898, English author,* Alice's Adventures in Wonderland, *"Down the Rabbit-Hole" (1865)*

Times are bad. Children no longer obey their parents, and everyone is writing a book.
CICERO, 106–43 BC

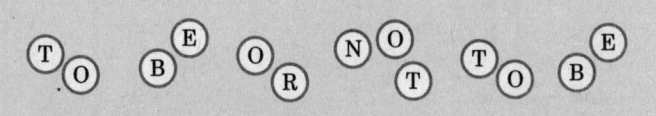

The Infinite Monkey Theory in popular culture is that if you get a million monkeys and give them a million typewriters, one or several of them would eventually come up with a Shakespeare play. They might also come up with *Madame Bovary, War and Peace* or *Tristram Shandy* while they are at it. Several experiments have tried to put this theory into practice, but none has come up with a masterpiece. It's probably only a question of time though.

A SURVEY RELEASED BY THE NATIONAL ENDOWMENT FOR THE ARTS ENTITLED READING AT RISK:

A Survey of Literary Reading in America, points to a dramatic decline in the number of adults reading literary fiction across the country. The biggest drop in readers was in the youngest age groups where a 28 percent decline was noticed between 1982 and 2002.

No place affords a more striking conviction of the vanity of human hopes, than a public library.
SAMUEL JOHNSON, 1709–1784, The Rambler *(1750)*

Top Pessimistic Books

Catcher in the Rye by J. D. Salinger
The Bell Jar by Sylvia Plath
Leviathan by Thomas Hobbes
The Stranger (L'Etranger) by Albert Camus
Molloy/Malone Dies/The Unnameable; trilogy by
   Samuel Beckett
The Road by Cormac McCarthy
The Trial by Franz Kafka
Anna Karenina by Leo Tolstoy

Lies and literature have always been friends.
JEAN DE LA FONTAINE, *1621–1695*, Fables, Contre ceux qui ont le
gout difficile *(1668)*

*You have to have something vicious in you to be a creative
writer . . . God save me from being 'nice.'*
D. H. LAWRENCE, *1885–1930, English writer, "Phoenix" (1927)*

BOREDOM

Dear World, I am leaving because I am bored . . . I am
leaving you with your worries in this sweet cesspool.
GEORGE SANDERS, *1906–1972, British actor, said to be the
opening line of the actor's suicide note*

If only people had the gift of knowing when they were bored and the courage to admit the fact openly when it was discovered, how many novelists, poets, playwrights, musicians and entertainers would be compelled to join the ranks of the unemployed?
ARNOLD BENNETT, Journals of Arnold Bennett *(1896–1910)*

Boredom, n: apathy, cheerlessness, dejection, disinterest, dispiritedness, dissatisfaction, drowsiness, dullness, total emptiness, ennui, fatigue, heaviness, immobility, indifference, inertia, laziness, lassitude, lethargy, lifelessness, listlessness, melancholia, passivity, sluggishness, spleen, tedium, unhappiness, weariness, and the list goes on, too boring to name them all.

The effect of boredom on a large scale has been underestimated. It is a main cause of revolutions and would soon bring to an end all static Utopias and the farmyard civilization of the Fabians.
WILLIAM RALPH INGE, 1860–1954, The End of an Age *(1948)*

Symmetry is boredom and boredom is the basis of grief. Despair yawns.
VICTOR HUGO, 1802–1885, Les Misérables *(1862)*

Since boredom advances and boredom is the root of all evil, no wonder, then, that the world goes backwards, that evil spreads. This can be traced back to the very beginning of the world. The gods were bored; therefore they created human beings.
SØREN KIERKEGAARD, 1813–1855, Danish philosopher

CHANGE

There is a certain relief in change, even though it be from bad to worse . . . I have often found in travelling in a stagecoach, that it is often a comfort to shift one's position and be bruised in a new place.

WASHINGTON IRVING, 1783–1859, Tales of a Traveller, *To the Reader (1824)*

Progress would be wonderful—if only it would stop.

ROBERT MUSIL, 1880–1942, Austrian writer

Change doth unknit the tranquil strength of men.

MATTHEW ARNOLD, 1822–1888, English social commentator

I believe we are on an irreversible trend toward more freedom and democracy—but that could change.

DAN QUAYLE, b. 1947, U.S. vice president

By the time a person has achieved years adequate for choosing a direction, the die is cast and the moment has long since passed which determined the future.

ZELDA FITZGERALD, 1900–1948, American novelist

What we call progress is the exchange of one nuisance for another nuisance.

HENRY HAVELOCK ELLIS, 1859–1939, British social reformer

It is easier to divert a river than change one's character.
Chinese proverb

Everyone thinks of changing the world, but no one thinks of changing himself.
LEO TOLSTOY, 1828–1910, Russian writer

All changes, even the most longed for, have their melancholy; for what we leave behind us is a part of ourselves; we must die to one life before we can enter another.
ANATOLE FRANCE, 1844–1924, French author

CIVILIZATION

You can't say civilization don't advance, however, for in every war they kill you in a new way.
WILL ROGERS, 1879–1935, New York Times (1929)

Every civilization that has ever existed has ultimately collapsed.
HENRY KISSINGER, b. 1923, New York Times (1974)

Why, as civilization spreads, do exceptional men become fewer?
ALEXIS DE TOCQUEVILLE, 1805–1859

When asked, circa 1930, what his view of Western civilization was, **Mahatma Gandhi** reportedly said, "I think it would be a good thing."

A Short History of Easter Island

When Europeans arrived on this tiny scrap of land in the middle of the Pacific, 1,300 miles from anywhere, in 1722, it was clear that the few degraded cannibals who lived there were the descendants of a great civilization who had built the famous, extraordinary, eighty-ton stone statues that look out to sea from the cliffs. What had happened? In a nutshell, the islanders had committed ecological suicide. They chopped down all their trees to act as rollers and levers for their statues, thereby deforesting their island to the extent that soil erosion killed off agriculture; over forty kinds of seabird could no longer nest there and so became extinct; palm fruits no longer grew; canoes could not be built for fishing; and there could be no more firewood. Does this all sound familiar? For eighty-ton statues, read Global Economy; for 10,000 people with axes, read 6 billion with bulldozers; for most remote habitable island in the world, read Planet Earth, alone in the galaxy . . .

As it will be in the future, it was at the birth of Man.
There are only four things certain since Social Progress began:—
That the Dog returns to his Vomit and the Sow returns to her Mire,
And the burnt Fool's bandaged finger goes wabbling back to the Fire.
RUDYARD KIPLING, *1865–1936, English author*

According to many, oil production has already peaked, is peaking, or will peak very soon. We can only guess at what this will mean for a civilization addicted to cheap oil. According to the U.S. Department of Energy's Hirsch report of 2005, peak oil presents the world with "an unprecedented risk management problem." It seems we do need to actually start doing something about the situation to avoid catastrophic upheaval, but so far the message from governments is: business as usual.

America is the only country in history that miraculously has gone directly from barbarism to decadence without the usual interval of civilisation.
GEORGES CLEMENCEAU, 1841–1929, French statesman

DEATH

There is . . . no death . . . There is only . . . me . . . me . . . who is going to die . . .
ANDRE MALRAUX, 1901–1976, French author, The Royal Way

Dying is a very dull, dreary affair. And my advice to you is to have nothing whatever to do with it.
W. SOMERSET MAUGHAM, 1874–1965, shortly before his death in 1965, as recorded by Robin Maugham

Any man's death diminishes me, because I am involved in mankind.

JOHN DONNE, 1572–1631, Meditation XVII

The graveyards are full of indispensable men.

CHARLES DE GAULLE, 1890–1970

Strange how sternly I am possessed of the idea that I shall not live much longer. Not a personal thought but is coloured with this conviction. I never look forward more than a year at the utmost; it is the habit of my mind, in utter sincerity, to expect no longer tenure of life than that. I don't know how this has come about; perhaps my absolute loneliness has something to do with it. Then I am haunted with the idea that I am consumptive. I never cough without putting a finger to my tongue, to see if there be a sign of blood. Morbidness—is it? I only know that these forecasts are the most essential feature of my mental and moral life at present. Death, if it came now, would rob me of not one hope, for hopes I simply have not.

GEORGE GISSING, 1857–1903, English novelist, Diary, *June 3, 1888*

A single death is a tragedy, a million deaths is a statistic.

JOSEF STALIN, 1879–1953

But in this world, nothing can be said
to be certain, except death and taxes.

BENJAMIN FRANKLIN, 1706–1790

If there wasn't death, I think you couldn't go on.

STEVIE SMITH, 1902–1971, The Observer *(1969)*

God is dead. (Nietzsche)
Nietzsche is dead. (God)
Graffito

The only choice then to be made is the most
aesthetically satisfying form of suicide: marriage,
and a forty-hour week; or a revolver.
ALBERT CAMUS, 1913–1960, Notebooks

DREAMS

Life is a dream; don't wake me!
Yiddish saying

We live as we dream—alone.
JOSEPH CONRAD, 1857–1924, Heart of Darkness

Life is perhaps most wisely regarded as a bad dream
between two awakenings . . .
EUGENE GLADSTONE O'NEILL, 1888–1953, Chu-Yin, Marco
Millions *(1928)*

He who looks too much at his dreams becomes like a
shadow.
Indian proverb

To believe in one's dreams is to spend all of one's life
asleep.
Chinese proverb

Heavy cheeses like **Stilton, Roquefort, and Gruyere** are
alleged by some to induce nightmares.

The hope I dreamed of was a dream,
Was but a dream; and now I wake,
Exceeding comfortless, and worn, and old,
For a dream's sake.
CHRISTINA ROSSETTI, *1830–1894, "Mirage" (1862)*

Night terrors are sleep disorders that occur in the first hour or so of sleep. Their cause isn't precisely known, but it is thought that they are perhaps due to excessive tiredness and anxiety. They lead to a wild state of confusion and disorientation that can be particularly alarming, for those witnessing the night terror as much as the sufferer. They most commonly occur in children aged two to six, with children kicking out and bucking violently, making unintelligible noises. Attempts to soothe a child in this state often fail and it is best to make sure they don't injure themselves.

DRUGS

Drugs are a waste of time. They destroy your memory and your self-respect and everything that goes along with your self-esteem.

KURT COBAIN, *1967–1994, American musician*

Have you ever seen the pictures of the wretched poet Coleridge? He smoked opium. Take a look at Coleridge, he was green about the gills and a stranger to the lavatory.

CLIFFORD MORTIMER warning his son John about constipatory effects of opium

The U.S. government's most recent National Survey on Drug Use and Health (2005) reported that over 800,000 American adolescents aged twelve to seventeen sold illegal drugs during the twelve months preceding the survey.

A study of 450 people published in 2008 by the National Institute of Drug Abuse in the United States found that smoking marijuana posed significant health risks to users. A study comparing 173 cancer patients and 176 healthy individuals produced evidence that marijuana smoking doubled or tripled the risk of developing cancer of the head or neck. Marijuana abuse also has the potential to promote cancer of the lungs and other parts of the respiratory tract because it produces 50–70 percent more carcinogenic hydrocarbons than tobacco smoke. Marijuana users usually inhale more deeply and hold their breath longer than tobacco smokers do, which increases the lungs' exposure to carcinogenic smoke.

Coca is a plant that the devil invented for the total destruction of the natives.

DON DIEGO DE ROBLES, 16th century Orthodox Catholic artist

In the 1970s and 1980s cocaine use in the United States increased more than 500 percent as the so-called War on Drugs began to reduce the amount of marijuana being smuggled into the States. Drug barons turned to cocaine and, to their delight, discovered it was easier to smuggle than cannabis and also yielded far higher profits for the volume smuggled. A second unintended consequence of the success against marijuana was that U.S. weed growers upped domestic production to meet demand and improved its quality (i.e., made it stronger) to compete with cocaine.

The United Nations' 2005 World Drug Report found that the global trade in illegal drugs generates more than $320 billion a year in revenues, which is higher than the GDP of 88% of the countries in the world.

£

Eighty percent of British banknotes—and 99 percent in London—are contaminated with cocaine or heroin and over 15 million pounds of the most dangerously contaminated have to be destroyed each year. Roughly 5 percent of cocaine users are thought to be infected with hepatitis C and leave traces of blood on the banknotes through which they snort the drug. Eight out of ten hepatitis C carriers are unaware they have the blood-carried virus, raising fears that infection rates will soar. Untreated, hepatitis C can lead to chronic liver disease.

EDUCATION

Tedium is the worst disease in schools, the corrupting tedium that comes equally from monotony, work or leisure.

RAUL D'AVILA, 1863–1895, Brazilian writer

It is the business of education to eliminate the influence of parents on the life-chances of the young.

F. MUSGROVE, The Family, Education, and Society *(1966)*

A real, honest, old-fashioned Boarding-school, where a reasonable quantity of accomplishments were sold at a reasonable price, and where girls might be sent to be out of the way and scramble themselves into a little education, without any danger of coming back prodigies.

JANE AUSTEN, 1775–1817, Emma *(1816)*

Education consists mainly in what we have unlearned.

MARK TWAIN, 1835–1910, American humorist

Nothing in this world can take the place of persistence. Talent will not; nothing is more common than unsuccessful people with talent. Genius will not; unrewarded genius is almost a proverb. Education will not; the world is full of educated derelicts.

CALVIN COOLIDGE, 1872–1933, U.S. president

In early 2008 a New Jersey librarian placed a sign in her computer room saying "Just say No to Wikipedia." Her campaign was picked up by other libraries who decided to block access to the online encyclopedia on their computers. The criticism of Wikipedia and search engines is that students are no longer studying anything, merely copying and pasting the first thing that pops up on their screens, without verifying sources or finding out the facts. What happened to students reading and studying till the small hours of the morning?

Democracy means government by the uneducated, while aristocracy means government by the badly educated.
G. K. CHESTERTON, 1874–1936, New York Times *(1931)*

Chi sa fa e chi non sa insegna.
Those who know, do, and those who don't, teach.
Italian proverb

You teach a child to read, and he or her will be able to pass a literacy test.
GEORGE W. BUSH, b. 1946, U.S. president

A good education is not so much one which prepares a man to succeed in the world, as one which enables him to sustain a failure.
BERNARD IDDINGS BELL, 1886–1958, Life, *October 16, 1950*

ENVIRONMENT

Nice Gaias Finish Last

According to the renowned scientist and originator of GAIA theory James Lovelock, *"We are on the edge of the greatest die-off humanity has ever seen. We will be lucky if 20 percent of us survive what is coming. We should be scared stiff . . . What we have lived through, the twentieth century, has been like a great party. Adults now have had the best time humanity has ever had. Now the party is over and the Earth is reckoning up."*

Lovelock was instrumental in discovering that CFC's were destroying the ozone layer. In *The Revenge of Gaia,* he asserts that the planet, which is a self-regulating and complex but single organism, is suffering from an illness—mankind, and that a tipping point has almost certainly been reached. The Earth will restabilize, but not in a way that favors civilization. Billions will die, and eventually a few breeding pairs of humans will migrate to the only places where the climate remains tolerable: Canada, Siberia, and the Arctic basin. Scorning the concept of "sustainable development," Lovelock suggests that "sustainable retreat" is now the only sensible option, if, indeed, we still have an option.

God forbid that India should ever take to industrialism after the manner of the west . . . keeping the world in chains. If our nation took to similar economic exploitation, it would strip the world bare like locusts.
MAHATMA GANDHI, 1869–1948

Only when the last tree has been cut down
Only after the last river has been poisoned
Only after the last fish has been caught
Only then will you find that money cannot be eaten
Cree Indian Prophecy

AT ANY MINUTE:

The Yellowstone National Park Super-Volcano Could Erupt

Last time this volcano erupted about 640,000 years ago, it covered North America in a layer of dust several feet deep. It is known to erupt every 600,000 to 700,000 years, so we're bang on schedule—and, according to some scientists, global warming only makes an eruption more likely. Apparently, the caldera underneath the volcano is filling up with magma, preparing for an almighty explosion whose force, it's estimated, could be similar to 1,000 Hiroshima-style atomic bombs *per second*, bringing on an interminable winter in which nothing grows and most life is extinguished.

A very few years ago, scientists assumed that the Earth's ice would take thousands of years to melt; now, it appears that the Arctic will be completely free of sea ice in summer within five or six years. So, what can we expect? The geological record shows that, 3 million years ago, when the temperature was five degrees more than it is now, sea levels were at least eighty feet higher.

Only about 4 percent of the world's oceans remain undamaged by human activity. The UN Environment Program estimates that every square mile of ocean contains 46,000 pieces of floating plastic—syringes, condoms, cigarette lighters—causing the deaths of more than a million seabirds and 100,000 marine mammals every year. There is now a ten-million-square-mile continent of plastic rubbish in the North Pacific Tropical Gyre held in place by swirling underwater currents; this "Great Pacific Garbage Patch" is just one of seven major tropical oceanic gyres where more and more Barbies and Kens, among other products of our consume-then-throw-away culture, gyrate forever.

FAME

Fame is a food that dead men eat,
I have no stomach for such meat.
HENRY AUSTIN DOBSON, 1840–1921, "Fame Is a Fool" (1906)

What I'd really like to say about stardom is that it gave
me everything I never wanted.
AVA GARDNER, 1922–1990, American actress, My Story *(1990)*

If you can't be famous, at least you can be notorious.
MOHAMAD MAHATHIR, b. 1925, Malaysia's longest-serving
prime minister

Fame and tranquility are two things that cannot stay
under the same roof.
MICHEL EYQUEM DE MONTAIGNE, 1533–1592, Essais

I want to be alone.
GRETA GARBO, 1905–1990, Swedish-born actress

John Lennon's killer, **Mark Chapman**, reportedly shot the
singer because he wanted to steal his fame from him. To a
certain degree, he did.

Throughout my life, I have seen narrow-shouldered men,
without a single exception, committing innumerable stupid acts, brutalizing their fellows and perverting souls by
all means. They call the motive for their actions fame.
COMTE DE LAUTRÉAMONT, 1846–1870

Once you become famous you get completely dehumanised. I think people forget there is a person in there trying to deal with it. . . . Partly the way you deal with it is by not reading, not looking and seeing any of it and burying your head in the sand. It is the only path to sanity.

KEIRA KNIGHTLEY, *b. 1985, quoted on BBC web interview*

Fame has also this great drawback, that if we pursue it, we must direct our lives so as to please the fancy of men.

BARUCH SPINOZA, *1632–1677, Dutch philosopher*

Fame is like a big piece of meringue—it's beautiful and you keep eating it, but it doesn't really fill you up.

Attributed to PIERCE BROSNAN, *b. 1953,* The Times *(2002)*

FAMILY

No family can hang out the sign, "Nothing the matter here."

Chinese proverb

Family! . . . the home of all social evil, a charitable institution for comfortable women, an anchorage for housefathers, and a hell for children.

AUGUST STRINDBERG, *1849–1912, Swedish dramatist,* The Son of a Servant *(1886)*

All happy families resemble one another, but each unhappy family is unhappy in its own way.
LEO TOLSTOY, *opening lines of* Anna Karenina *(1873)*

Heads, heads! . . . five children—mother—tall lady, eating sandwiches—forgot the arch—crash—knock—children look round—mother's head off—sandwich in her hand—no mouth to put it in—head of a family off—shocking, shocking!
CHARLES DICKENS, The Pickwick Papers *(1836–1837)*

We have a country governed by blockheads and knaves; the ties of marriage with all its felicity are severed and destroyed; our wives and daughters are thrown to the stews; our children are cast into the world from the breast and forgotten; filial piety is extinguished; and our surnames, the only mark of distinction among families, are abolished. Can the imagination paint anything more dreadful on this side of hell?
TIMOTHY DWIGHT, *1752–1817, American theologian*

Peter remained on friendly terms with Christ notwithstanding Christ's having healed his mother-in-law.
SAMUEL BUTLER, *1835–1902, English writer*

If a man's character is to be abused, say what you will, there's nobody like a relation to do the business.
WILLIAM MAKEPEACE THACKERAY, *1811–1863, English novelist,* Vanity Fair *(1847)*

The most dangerous word in any human tongue is the word for brother. It's inflammatory.
TENNESSEE WILLIAMS, *1911–1983,* Camino Real *(1953)*

FAMOUS LAST WORDS

Doctor, do you think it could have been the sausage?
PAUL CLAUDEL, 1868–1955, French composer

I should never have switched from Scotch to Martinis.
HUMPHREY BOGART, 1899–1957, American actor

Everything has gone wrong, my girl.
ARNOLD BENNETT, 1867–1931, English novelist

It wasn't worth it.
LOUIS B. MAYER, 1882–1957, film producer

I'm bored with it all.
WINSTON CHURCHILL, 1874–1965

Suicide note:

And so I leave this world, where the heart must either break or turn to lead.
SEBASTIÉN-ROCH NICOLAS DE CHAMFORT, 1741–1794

To his confessor:

What the devil are you trying to sing, monsieur le curé? Your voice is out of tune.
JEAN-PHILIPPE RAMEAU, 1683–1764, French composer

I am a Queen, but I have not the power to move my arms.
LOUISE, QUEEN OF PRUSSIA, 1776–1810

As the lamp by his bed flared up:

What? The flames already?
VOLTAIRE, 1694–1778

Only one man ever understood me . . . And he didn't understand me.
GEORG WILHELM FRIEDRICH HEGEL, 1770–1831, German philosopher

I knew it. I knew it. Born in a hotel room—and God damn it—died in a hotel room.
EUGENE O'NEILL, 1888–1953, American playwright

On his deathbed:

I have spent a lot of time searching through the Bible for loopholes.
W. C. FIELDS, 1879–1946, American actor

This is absurd! This is absurd!
SIGMUND FREUD, 1856–1939

Go on, get out! Last words are for fools who haven't said enough!
KARL MARX, 1818–1883

FASHION

Beware all enterprises that require new clothes.
HENRY DAVID THOREAU, 1817–1862, Walden, or Life in the
Woods, *"Economy" (1854)*

Fashion is more tyrannical at Paris than in any other
place in the world; it governs even more absolutely than
their king, which is saying a great deal. The least revolt
against it is punished by proscription. You must observe
and conform to all the minutiae of it, if you will be in
fashion there yourself; and if you are not in fashion, you
are nobody.
*FOURTH EARL OF CHESTERFIELD, 1694–1773, Letter to his son
(1750)*

Proposals to ban saggy trousers that reveal too much
underwear are underway in some American cities. The
fashion began as a way of mimicking prison clothes
where the absence of belts and braces (in case of hanging, self-harm, or violence) means that clothes often
hang loose. It seems the process has come full circle as
many lawmakers are proposing that citizens revealing
too much buttock in the street can now be fined or end
up in jail.

Intense debate still surrounds the effects of the fashion industry's emphasis on size zero models and the high incidences of anorexia nervosa and bulimia in industrialized countries. While some in the fashion industry, as in Spain, are adapting shop mannequins to larger sizes and thinking about banning stick-thin catwalk models, others deny the link vehemently. Suffice to say that anorexia nervosa has one of the highest mortality rates for any mental disorder; between 5 and 20 percent of those with the disorder don't survive the complications the disease brings.

Fashion victims are not just people who want to wear the latest styles. According to the organization PETA, 85 percent of the fur industry's skins come from animals brought up in captivity. The most farmed fur animals are minks and foxes. Rabbits, chinchillas, and lynxes are also used. Killing methods vary, but the ultimate aim is to keep the animals' skins and pelts unblemished. This means that poisoning, genital electrocution, gassing and decompression chambers, and neck breaking are all methods used on a regular basis. For animals captured in the wild the process can be even more brutal.

And it is a wonder what will be the fashion after the plague is done as to periwigs, for nobody will dare to buy any haire for fear of the infection—that it had been cut off the heads of people dead of the plague.
SAMUEL PEPYS, *1633–1703, English diarist*

Fashion condemns us to many follies; the greatest is to make ourselves its slave.
NAPOLEON BONAPARTE, *1769–1821*

Fashion, n: A despot whom the wise ridicule and obey.
AMBROSE BIERCE, 1842–c.1914, The Devil's Dictionary *(1911)*

FOOD

He who eats alone chokes alone.
Proverb

- **Roughly 800 million people in the world are malnourished.**
- **One child dies every five seconds through malnutrition and related causes.**
- **Two hundred million children are underweight.**
- **There is enough food to feed the world.**
  UN's World Food Program facts

Over a billion people worldwide are overweight and at least 300 million obese.
WORLD HEALTH ORGANIZATION

Vegetarians have wicked, shifty eyes, and laugh in a cold calculating manner. They pinch little children, steal stamps, drink water, favour beards.
J. B. MORTON, 1893–1979, Daily Express *(British tabloid)*

If only it was as easy to banish hunger by rubbing the belly as it is to masturbate.
DIOGENES THE CYNIC, Greek philosopher

I'm frightened of eggs; worse than frightened, they revolt me. That white round thing without any holes—have you ever seen anything more revolting than an egg yolk breaking and spilling its yellow liquid? Blood is jolly, red. But egg yolk is yellow, revolting. I've never tasted it.

ALFRED HITCHCOCK, *1899–1980, film director*

We have been shocked to find that very large quantities of GM (animal) feed are being used in the UK to produce our food. Around 60% of the maize and 30% of the soya is GM in the feed used by dairy and pig farmers. This means that most of the non-organic milk, dairy products and pork being sold in the UK is from GM-fed animals.

Soil Association investigation in 2007

The English who eat their meat red and bloody, show the savagery that goes with such food.

J.O. DE LA METTRIE, *1709–1751, French physician*

FRIENDSHIP

Whenever a friend succeeds, a little something inside me dies.

GORE VIDAL, *b. 1925, American writer*

No one ever really minds seeing a friend fall from a high roof.

CONFUCIUS, *551–479 BC, Chinese philosopher*

In the misfortune of our best friends, we always find something which is not displeasing to us.
Duc de la Rochefoucauld, 1613–1680

Friendship, n. A ship big enough to carry two in fair weather; but only one in foul.
Ambrose Bierce, 1842–c.1914, The Devil's Dictionary *(1911)*

Few friendships would endure if each party knew what his friend said about him in his absence, even when speaking sincerely and dispassionately.
Blaise Pascal, 1623–1662, mathematician

It is difficult to say who do you the worst mischief, enemies with the worst intentions or friends with the best.
Edward Bulwer-Lytton, 1803–1873, British novelist

One friend in a lifetime is much; two are many; three are hardly possible.
Henry Brooks Adams, 1838–1918, American historian

In 2007, the number of people visiting social networking sites such as MySpace and Facebook was into the hundreds of millions. Indeed, according to a recent report, 40 percent of adults in the UK regularly visit these sites to meet "like-minded" people. However, before inviting total strangers into your life, albeit online, you might want to consider the following: You are a part of the greatest forum for advertising ever known.

Old friendships are, like meats served up repeatedly, cold, comfortless, and distasteful. The stomach turns against them. Either constant intercourse and familiarity breed weariness and contempt; or, if we meet again after an interval of absence, we appear no longer the same. One is too wise, another too foolish, for us; and we wonder we did not find this out before. We are disconcerted and kept in a state of continual alarm by the wit of one, or tired to death of the dullness of another. . . . The most amusing or instructive companion is at best like a favourite volume, that we wish after a time to *lay upon the shelf*; but as our friends are not willing to be laid there, this produces a misunderstanding and ill-blood between us.

WILLIAM HAZLITT, *"On the Pleasure of Hating,"* Table Talk *(1822)*

But of all plagues, good Heaven, thy wrath can send,
Save me, oh save me, from the candid friend.

GEORGE CANNING, *1770–1827, British prime minister*

FUTURE

Why should I care about posterity? What's posterity ever done for me?

GROUCHO MARX, *1890–1977, American comedian*

If you want a picture of the future, imagine a boot stamping on a human face—forever.

GEORGE ORWELL, *1903–1950,* Nineteen Eighty-Four *(1948)*

I would sum up my fear about the future in one word: boring. And that's my one fear: that everything has happened; nothing exciting or new or interesting is ever going to happen again . . . the future is just going to be a vast, conforming suburb of the soul.

J. G. BALLARD, b. 1930, British author

The Ten Threats Identified by the High Level Threat Panel set up by the United Nations in 2003 are the following:

Poverty
Infectious disease
Environmental degradation
Inter-state war
Civil war
Genocide
Other atrocities (sexual slavery, or kidnapping for body parts)
Proliferation of weapons of mass destruction
Terrorism
Transnational organized crime

Colin Mason's 2006 book, *A Short History of the Future*, focuses on six powerful "drivers" which, converging in about twenty years time, could plunge the world into a new Dark Age. The drivers are: peak oil, massive population growth, global climate change, poverty, famine and water shortages, and the breakdown of international law and order.

An oceanic island volcano collapse could trigger a mega-tsunami

The western flank of the Cumbre Vieja volcano on the island of La Palma in the Canaries is starting to slide seawards. Research suggests that eventually a gigantic mass of rock will plunge into the ocean. This monstrous landslide will (we hope) give us warning that it's about to occur, but in any case the event will be catastrophic, producing massive waves and striking the entire western seaboard of the Atlantic a few hours after the Splash. *Ate a vista*, Rio de Janeiro! *So long*, New York!

GOODBYE, SUN

Theories about how the universe will end include "The Big Crunch," where it stops expanding and shrinks into a black hole, and "The Big Rip," where it's torn apart by its own continued expansion, with galaxies separating from each other, the solar system falling apart, stars and planets being ripped asunder and, finally, in the last instant, atoms being destroyed. But, no matter—it will all be over for life on Earth long before any of these scenarios are played out. In about five billion years, the sun will exhaust its supply of hydrogen and evolve into a red giant, becoming hugely bigger than it is now. The extra heat will almost certainly boil the Earth's oceans, causing all our water to evaporate; and the atmosphere will disintegrate shortly before the rock begins to melt. In the unlikely event of us surviving this heat-stroke, we will die of cold when the sun eventually turns into a white dwarf, and gives off no heat at all.

I've buried a time-capsule containing large samples of dynamite, gunpowder and nitroglycerine. It's set to go off in the year 3000. That should show people living in the future what we are really like.

ALFRED HITCHCOCK, 1899–1980, film director

GENIUS

I hate everything approaching temperamental inspiration, "sacred fire" and all those attributes of genius which serve only as cloaks for untidy minds.

PIET MONDRIAN, 1872–1944, quoted in F. Elgar, Mondrian *(1968)*

There is in every madman a misunderstood genius whose idea, shining in his head, frightened people, and for whom delirium was the only solution to the strangulation that life had prepared for him.

ANTONIN ARTAUD, 1896–1948, French playwright

Every positive value has its price in negative terms ... The genius of Einstein leads to Hiroshima.

Attributed to PABLO PICASSO, 1881–1973

Art is a jealous mistress, and if a man have a genius for painting, poetry, music, architecture, or philosophy, he makes a bad husband and an ill provider.

RALPH WALDO EMERSON, 1803–1882, The Conduct of Life, *"Wealth" (1860)*

Savant syndrome is a rare condition in which people display serious mental or physical disability as well as spectacular talent or genius. People with this condition have been disparagingly described as "idiot savants." Sufferers typically might have difficulty tying their shoelaces but can provide an accurate drawing of a building in a few minutes.

Genius is sorrow's child.

JOHN ADAMS, 1735–1826

There are two paths in life: one is the regular one, direct, honest. The other is bad, it leads through death—that is the way of genius!

THOMAS MANN, 1875–1955, The Magic Mountain *(1924)*

The difference between stupidity and genius is that genius has its limits.

Attributed to ALBERT EINSTEIN, 1879–1955

John Forbes Nash, born 1928, was a Cold War strategist and winner of the 1994 Nobel Prize for economics. Recognized as a mathematical genius, he spiraled downward into paranoid schizophrenia at the age of thirty. His remarkable powers were brought to life in an award-winning book by Sylvia Nasar and in the 2001 film, *A Beautiful Mind,* by Akiva Goldsman, starring Russell Crowe.

Genius is one percent inspiration and ninety-nine percent perspiration.
Thomas Edison, 1847–1931, Harper's Monthly *(1932)*

It takes a lot of time to be a genius, you have to sit around so much doing nothing, really doing nothing.
Gertrude Stein, 1874–1946, Everybody's Autobiography *(1937)*

The public is wonderfully tolerant. It forgives everything except genius.
Oscar Wilde, 1854–1900

HEALTH

Cured yesterday of my disease,
I died last night of my physician.
Matthew Prior, 1664–1721, "The Remedy worse than the disease" *(1727)*

Nothing is more fatal to health, than an over care of it.
Benjamin Franklin, 1706–1790

A child dies of malaria every thirty seconds. Malaria kills over a million people each year and is second only to tuberculosis in its impact on world health. The disease, spread by mosquitoes, is endemic in ninety countries and every year roughly 600 million people, or one person in every ten on the planet, become severely ill with malaria. Malaria is both preventable and curable.

Experts at World Health Organization and elsewhere believe that the world is now closer to a flu pandemic than at any time since 1968, when the last of the previous century's three pandemics occurred. Scientists now believe the Spanish flu virus of 1918/19, which killed 40 million people around the world in a matter of months, came from birds and bore similarities to the avian flu that has emerged in recent years. A global flu pandemic would kill between seven million and 200 million, depending on which scientist or medical journal you read.

It may seem a strange principle to enunciate as the very first requirement of a Hospital that it should do the sick no harm.
FLORENCE NIGHTINGALE, 1820–1910, Notes on Hospitals *(1863)*

Louis Pasteur's theory of germs is ridiculous fiction.
PIERRE PACHET, professor of physiology at Toulouse (1872)

The number of people living with HIV/AIDS has risen from around 8 million in 1990 to more than 33 million today, and continues to grow. Africa has 12 million AIDS orphans. People under twenty-five years old account for half of all new HIV infections worldwide. In 2007, it claimed the lives of an estimated 2 million people, including 330,000 children. More than 25 million people have died of AIDS since 1981.

Be careful about reading health books. You may die of a misprint.
MARK TWAIN, 1835–1910, American humorist

A few bumper stickers to keep your mind on the road

- You're never alone with schizophrenia.
- I used to be mental, but we're OK now.
- Out of my mind. Back in five minutes.
- Are the voices in my head bothering you?

Heart attacks, strokes, and diabetes kill about 20 million people every year, more than are killed by war, famine, AIDS, tuberculosis, and malaria combined, and more than might conceivably be killed in a single pandemic of bird flu.
WORLD HEALTH ORGANIZATION

Eat right, exercise regularly, die anyway.
Author unknown

HISTORY

For four-fifths of our history, our planet was populated by pond scum.

J. W. SCHOPF, paleobiologist

It has been said that although God cannot alter the past, historians can—it is perhaps because they can be useful to Him in this respect that He tolerates their existence.

SAMUEL BUTLER, 1835–1902, English writer

Men heap together the mistakes of their lives, and create a monster they call Destiny.

JOHN OLIVER HOBBES, pen name of English novelist Pearl Richards Craigie, 1867–1906

Happy the people whose annals are blank in history books!

THOMAS CARLYLE, 1795–1881, Scottish essayist

History is more or less bunk.

HENRY FORD, 1863–1947, founder of Ford Motor Company

Indeed, history is no more than a tableau of crimes and misfortunes.

VOLTAIRE, 1694–1778

History is the short trudge from Adam to atom.
Leonard Louis Levinson, 1905–1974, American anthologist

Those who compare the age in which their lot has fallen
with a golden age which exists only in imagination, may
talk of degeneracy and decay; but no man who is cor-
rectly informed as to the past, will be disposed to take a
morose or desponding view of the present.
Thomas Babington Macaulay, 1800–1859, English historian

HUMAN NATURE

We:

. . . are born between shit and piss.
St. Augustine of Hippo, 354–430

. . . are born crying, live complaining and die disappointed.
Doctor Thomas Fuller, Gnomologia *(1732)*

. . . are just statistics, born to consume resources.
Horace, 65–8 BC, Epistles

. . . are all of us sentenced to solitary confinement inside
our own skins, for life.
Tennessee Williams, 1911–1983, Orpheus Descending *(1957)*

There is no such thing as inner peace. There is only nervousness or death.

FRAN LEBOWITZ, b. 1950, U.S. author, Metropolitan Life *(1978)*

Anyone informed that the universe is expanding and contracting in pulsations of eighty billion years has a right to ask, "What's in it for me?"

PETER DE VRIES, 1910–1993, U.S. novelist, The Glory of the Hummingbird *(1974)*

How did I get into the world? Why was I not asked about it and why was I not informed of the rules and regulations but just thrust into the ranks as if I had been bought from a peddling shanghaier of human beings? How did I get involved in this big enterprise called actuality? Why should I be involved?

SØREN KIERKEGAARD, 1813–1855, Danish philosopher, Fear and Trembling *(1843)*

I don't believe in the infinite importance of man. I see no reason to believe that a shudder would go through the sky if the whole ant-heap were kerosened.

F. R. LEAVIS, 1895–1978, British literary critic

Drinking when we are not thirsty and making love all year round, madam; that is all there is to distinguish us from other animals.

PIERRE-AUGUSTIN CARON DE BEAUMARCHAIS, 1732–1799, French dramatist, Le Mariage de Figaro *(1785)*

The people only anxiously desire two things: bread and the Circus games.

Juvenal, late first–early second century AD, Roman poet, Satires

The Stanford Prison Experiment

In 1971, Philip Zimbardo, of Stanford University, wanted to do a psychological study of the behavioral effects of captivity on prisoners and prison guards. Undergraduates volunteered to play the role of both guards and prisoners and to live for two weeks in a mock prison in the Stanford psychology building basement. However, the experiment went well beyond what had been predicted, and, with the guards becoming increasingly sadistic, had to be brought to an end after a mere six days.

If one looks with a cold eye at the mess man has made of his history, it is difficult to avoid the conclusion that he has been afflicted by some built-in mental disorder which drives him towards self-destruction.

Arthur Koestler, 1905–1983, British writer, in The Observer, *1968*

If the whole human race lay in one grave, the epitaph on the headstone might well be, "It seemed a good idea at the time".

Rebecca West, 1892–1983, Irish writer

KINDNESS

It is really very disheartening how we depend on other people in this life.
ROBERT LOUIS STEVENSON, 1850–1894

One of the worst things about life is not how nasty the nasty people are. You know that already. It is how nasty the nice people can be.
ANTHONY POWELL, 1905–2000, English novelist, Hearing Secret Harmonies *(1975)*

To see others suffer does one good, to make others suffer even more: this is a hard saying but an ancient, mighty, human, all-too-human principle to which even the apes might subscribe; for it has been said that in devising bizarre cruelties they anticipate man and are, as it were, his "prelude." Without cruelty there is no festival . . .
FRIEDRICH NIETZSCHE, 1844–1900, German philosopher, The Genealogy of Morals *(1887)*

Wherever a man goes, men will pursue him and paw him with their dirty institutions, and, if they can, constrain him to belong to their desperate oddfellow society.
HENRY DAVID THOREAU, 1817–1862, Walden *(1854)*

We must love one another, yes, yes, that's all true enough, but nothing says we have to like each other.
PETER DE VRIES, 1910–1993, American novelist, The Glory of the Hummingbird *(1974)*

I do not want people to be very agreeable, as it saves me the trouble of liking them a good deal.
JANE AUSTEN, 1775–1817, letter to her sister Cassandra, 1798

I wish I loved the Human Race;
I wish I loved its silly face;
I wish I liked the way it walks;
I wish I liked the way it talks;
And when I'm introduced to one
I wish I thought What Jolly Fun!

WALTER ALEXANDER RALEIGH, 1861–1922, essayist, Laughter from a Cloud *(1923)*

Hell is other people.
JEAN-PAUL SARTRE, 1905–1980, No Exit *(1944)*

Have you ever thought what a fine world this would be if it weren't for the people in it?
EDEN PHILPOTTS, 1862–1960, English novelist

LAW & LAWYERS

Woe unto you, lawyers! For ye have taken away the key of knowledge.
Luke 11:52

Lawyers' houses are built on the heads of fools.
GEORGE HERBERT, 1593–1633, poet, Jacula Prudentum *(1651)*

Dice are small polka-dotted cubes of ivory, constructed like a lawyer to lie on any side.
AMBROSE BIERCE, *1842–c.1914*, The Devil's Dictionary

A learned gentleman who rescues your estate from your enemies . . . and keeps it for himself.
LORD BROUGHAM, *1778–1868, British writer and statesman, of a lawyer*

The first thing we do, let's kill all the lawyers.
WILLIAM SHAKESPEARE, *1564–1616*, King Henry VI, Part ii

We all know here that the law is the most powerful of schools for the imagination. No poet ever interpreted nature as freely as a lawyer interprets the truth.
JEAN GIRAUDOUX, *1882–1944, French writer*, Tiger at the Gates *(1935)*

It usually takes a hundred years to make a law; and then, after it has done its work, takes a hundred to get rid of it.
HENRY WARD BEECHER, *1813–1887, American clergyman and campaigner*, Life Thoughts *(1858)*

A jury is composed of twelve men of average ignorance.
HERBERT SPENCER, *1820–1903, English philosopher*

A man may as well open an oyster without a knife as a lawyer's mouth without a fee.
BARTEN HOLYDAY, *1593–1661, English clergyman and poet*

The one great principle of the English law is to make business for itself.
CHARLES DICKENS, *1812–1870, English novelist*, Bleak House *(1853)*

PROVERBS

A MAN WHO IS HIS OWN LAWYER HAS A FOOL FOR HIS CLIENT.

IT IS BETTER TO BE A MOUSE IN A CAT'S MOUTH THAN A MAN
IN A LAWYER'S HANDS.

THE DEVIL MAKES HIS CHRISTMAS PIES OF LAWYERS' TONGUES
AND CLERKS' FINGERS.

LIFE

You fall out of your mother's womb, you crawl across open country under fire, and you drop into your grave.
QUENTIN CRISP, 1908–1999, from An Evening with Quentin Crisp

There are only three events in a man's life; birth, life and death; he is unaware of being born, he dies in pain, and he forgets to live.
JEAN DE LA BRUYERE, 1645–1696, French essayist

What do baths bring to your mind? Oil, sweat, dirt, greasy water and everything that is disgusting. Such, then, is life in all its parts and such is every material thing in it.
MARCUS AURELIUS, 121–180, Roman Emperor, Meditations

The world is a grindstone and life is your nose.
FRED ALLEN, 1894–1956, American humorist

Most people get a fair amount of fun out of their lives, but on balance life is suffering and only the very young or the very foolish imagine otherwise.
GEORGE ORWELL, 1903–1950, "Shooting an Elephant" (1950)

LIFE IS

. . . a cheap table d'hote in a rather dirty restaurant, with time changing the plates before you've had enough of anything.
THOMAS KETTLE, 1880–1916, Irish poet

. . . everywhere a state in which much is to be endured, and little to be enjoyed.

SAMUEL JOHNSON, *1709–1784*, Rasselas (*1759*)

. . . just one damned thing after another.

ELBERT HUBBARD, *1856–1915, American writer and philosopher*

It is not true that life is one damn thing after another—it is one damn thing over and over.

EDNA ST. VINCENT MILLAY, *1892–1950, American poet*

Time is a great teacher, they say. Unfortunately, it kills all its pupils.

HECTOR BERLIOZ, *1803–1869, French composer*

O_2

All day, every day, we breathe in a highly toxic substance which leads to the production of free radicals in our systems. These, in turn, sometimes cause damage to our DNA which may, occasionally, result in the formation of a tumor. This chain of events is statistically likely to happen over a long period of time, so, as we live for longer and longer lifespans, more and more of us will get cancer. Already, it's one in three. But it's no use trying to avoid inhaling the noxious stuff that will get us in the end: it's called *oxygen*.

Who would venture on the journey of life if compelled to begin it at the end?

MME DE MAINTENON, *1635–1719, wife of Louis XIV*

Life can then little else supply
But a few good fucks and then we die.
THOMAS POTTER, An Essay on Woman *(1755)*

LOVE

I can understand companionship. I can understand bought sex in the afternoon. What I cannot understand is the love affair.

GORE VIDAL, *b. 1925, American writer, in* The Sunday Times *(London), 1973*

WHAT IS LOVE, ANYWAY?

. . . the desire to prostitute oneself. There is, indeed, no exalted pleasure that cannot be related to prostitution.

CHARLES BAUDELAIRE, *1821–1867, French poet,* Intimate Journals *(1887)*

. . . the desire of satisfying a voracious appetite with a certain quantity of delicate white human flesh.

HENRY FIELDING, *1707–1754,* Tom Jones *(1749)*

. . . a sin in theology, a forbidden intercourse in jurisprudence, a mechanical insult in medicine, and a subject philosophy has no time for.

KARL KRAUS, *1874–1936, Austrian satirist*

Ten Country-Western Songs

- I Liked You Better Before I Got to Know You So Well
- How Can I Miss You If You Won't Go Away?
- It's Hard to Kiss the Lips at Night That Chewed Your Ass Out All Day Long
- She Got The Ring and I Got the Finger
- You're the Reason Our Kids Are Ugly
- If I Can't Be Number One in Your Life, Then Number Two on You
- I'm So Miserable Without You, It's Like You're Still Here
- If The Phone Don't Ring, You'll Know It's Me
- I Still Miss You Baby, But My Aim's Gettin' Better
- If I Had Shot You When I First Wanted To, I'd Be Out of Prison by Now

We all know that romantic, passionate love doesn't last, but surely the "companionate" love it turns into is the real thing—a long-term emotion that only grows as couples stay together through thick and thin? Not so, according to psychology professor Elaine Hatfield at the University of Hawaii. After a series of interviews with nearly 1,000 couples, she and her fellow social psychologist Jane Traupmann presented their findings that, contrary to prevailing wisdom, companionate love declines as precipitously as romantic love, and never stops declining.

Love is the fart
Of every heart:
It pains a man when 'tis kept close,
And others doth offend, when 'tis let loose.
JOHN SUCKLING, *1609–1642, English poet, "Love's Offence"*

Love seeketh only Self to please,
To bind another to its delight,
Joys in another's loss of ease,
And builds a Hell in Heaven's despite.
WILLIAM BLAKE, *1757–1827, "The Clod and the Pebble" (1794)*

Greeting an ex-lover after several years:

I thought I told you to wait in the car.
TALLULAH BANKHEAD, *1902–1968, American actress*

MARRIAGE

- A man without a wife is a man without a master.
- Neither marriage nor war will go away once begun.
- He who has a wife has pain.

Italian proverbs

I know nothing about sex because I was always married.
ZSA ZSA GABOR, *b. 1917, Hungarian-born American actress*

The most happy marriage I can picture or imagine to myself would be the union of a deaf man to a blind woman.

SAMUEL TAYLOR COLERIDGE, *1772–1834, English poet*

The widow/widower effect is the term coined to describe the trend whereby healthy spouses die soon after their wives or husbands. New findings from the University of Pennsylvania, published in the *New England Journal of Medicine,* prove that this is very real.

I NEVER KNEW WHAT REAL HAPPINESS WAS UNTIL
I GOT MARRIED; AND THEN IT WAS TOO LATE

LOVE MAY BE BLIND, BUT MARRIAGE
IS A REAL EYE-OPENER

MY OTHER WIFE IS BEAUTIFUL

NO HUSBAND HAS EVER BEEN SHOT
WHILE DOING THE DISHES

Bumper stickers

Vienna, Austria, has a phenomenally high divorce rate: 69 percent. The city, therefore, has decided to hold a first **Divorce Fair** to enable people to meet the right lawyers, estate agents, travel agents, counselors, and so on. Sunday's fair is open to women and Saturday's to men.

Shortest Celebrity Marriages

How short can a Hollywood or celebrity marriage be? Some are chasing annulment just a few hours after getting hitched.

Elizabeth Taylor and Nicky Hilton—8 months
Lisa Marie Presley and Nicolas Cage—3 months, 15 days
Drew Barrymore and Jeremy Thomas—30 days
Cher and Gregg Allman—9 days
Rudolph Valentino and Jean Acker—6 hours

- He that has a wife, has strife.
- A dead wife's the best goods in a man's house.

According to Charles L. Nunn of the **Department of Biology at the University of Virginia**, mammals that are monogamous or have small harem groups are more prone to extinction. Several duiker species which are monogamous died out around ten years after reserves had been set up for them in Ghana. The African buffalo, however, which has harems of about fifteen females, is still thriving in those reserves: "The most sexually active species . . . may have evolved elevated immune systems as a defense mechanism against disease. . . . We looked at animal species with a range of mating behaviors and found a strong relationship between high white blood cell counts and high promiscuity in healthy animals."

In Kebbi State, northern Nigeria, the average age of marriage for girls is just over eleven years, against a national average of seventeen.

When a man opens the car door for his wife, it's either a new car or a new wife.
Attributed to PRINCE PHILIP, b. 1921, Duke of Edinburgh

MEDIA

Trying to determine what is going on in the world by reading newspapers is like trying to tell the time by watching the second hand of a clock.
BEN HECHT, 1894–1964, American playwright and screenwriter

Theoretically, television may be feasible, but I consider it an impossibility—a development which we should waste little time dreaming about.
LEE DE FOREST, 1873–1961, inventor of the cathode ray tube

The pen is mightier than the sword if the sword is very short, and the pen is very sharp.
TERRY PRATCHETT, b. 1948, English author

A newspaper consists of the same number of words whether there be any news in it or not.
HENRY FIELDING, 1707–1754, author

You can't take something off the Internet—it's like taking piss out of a swimming pool.
Author unknown

Television? No good will come of this device. The word is half Greek and half Latin.
C. P. SCOTT, *1846–1932, editor*

If one morning I walked on top of the water across the Potomac River, the headline that afternoon would read: President Can't Swim.
LYNDON B. JOHNSON, *1908–1973, U.S. president*

The wireless music box has no imaginable commercial value. Who would pay for a message sent to nobody in particular?
Response of colleagues to a call from DAVID SARNOFF, *American pioneer of broadcast media, to invest in commercial radio in the 1920s*

My work is being destroyed almost as soon as it is printed. One day it is being read; the next day someone's wrapping fish in it.
AL CAPP, *1909–1979, American cartoonist*

There is practically no chance communications space satellites will be used to provide better telephone, telegraph, television, or radio service inside the United States.
T. CRAVEN, *U.S. Federal Communications commissioner, in 1961; the first commercial communications satellite went into service in 1965*

It's estimated that about 1.4 blogs are created every second of every day. Since online sources of information on every subject under the sun can be constantly updated, our daily papers risk being out-of-date in more ways than one. Will newsprint survive the onslaught of the digital age?

MEN

There are two good men: one dead, the other unborn.
Chinese proverb

Men first feel necessity, then look for utility, next attend to comfort, still later amuse themselves with pleasure, thence grow dissolute in luxury, and finally go mad and waste their substance.
GIAMBATTISTA VICO, 1668–1744, Italian philosopher

What is man, when you come to think upon him, but a minutely set, ingenious machine for turning, with infinite artfulness, the red wine of Shiraz into urine?
ISAK DINESEN, 1885–1962, Danish writer, "The Dreamers" (1935)

A single sentence will suffice for modern man: he fornicated and read the papers.
ALBERT CAMUS, 1913–1960

Between the ages of fifteen and twenty-four, with the onset of the "testosterone storm," males are nearly five times more likely to die than females. It comes as no surprise to find that most of these deaths are from car accidents followed by homicide, suicide, cancer, and death by drowning. The difference between men and women then narrows until after fifty-five when, again, more men than women die, thanks to heart disease (five in a thousand), suicide, car accidents, and smoking and drinking. And, finally, when male and female get old, men will, on average, die five years younger than women do. Is that all? No. Men are about five times more likely than women to be struck by lightning.

He is the most ridiculous beast on earth and the reason is his mind and his pudendum.
EDWARD DAHLBERG, 1900–1977, American novelist

A man is two people, himself and his cock. A man always takes his friend to the party. Of the two, the friend is the nicer, being more able to show his feelings.
BERYL BAINBRIDGE, b. 1934, British author

There is, of course, no reason for the existence of the male sex except that one sometimes needs help with moving the piano.
REBECCA WEST, 1892–1983, Irish writer, Sunday Telegraph, *1970*

In the new code of laws which I suppose it will be necessary for you to make I desire you would remember the ladies, and be more generous and favorable to them than your ancestors. Do not put such unlimited power into the hands of the husbands. Remember all men would be tyrants if they could.

First Lady ABIGAIL ADAMS, 1797–1801, letter to her husband John Adams, 1776

Men plant the seeds of their own obsolescence

Until recently, men (not just male scientists) were the only ones who could make spermatozoa. But, in 2007, scientists discovered a way of making sperm cells from bone marrow, thereby opening up the possibility of a woman making sperm from her own bone marrow and fertilizing another woman's egg—or vice versa—and leaving men neatly out of the equation. Redundancy beckons, and probably no severance package.

The man who has cured himself of BO and halitosis, has learned French to surprise the waiter, and the saxophone to amuse the company, may find that people still avoid him because they do not like him.

HEYWOOD BROUN, 1888–1939, American journalist

The more I see of men, the more I like dogs.

Attributed to various French women of the 18th century

MIDDLE AGE

Fair, fat and forty.
SIR WALTER SCOTT, 1771–1832, St. Ronan's Well (1823)

In the middle of the journey of our life
I found myself in a dark wood
Where the straight path was lost.
DANTE ALIGHIERI, Divina Commedia, *Inferno, Canto 1 (c. 1320)*

Faced with the collapse of his marriage, a forty-four-year-old Australian from Perth is planning to auction his life (his house, his job, his clothes, his friends) on eBay. By throwing out everything from his car to his friends, Ian Usher is planning to get rid of the chaos and the midlife blues that have beset his life and start again.

Everybody has a talent at twenty-five. The difficult thing is to have it at fifty.
EDGAR DEGAS, 1834–1917, French artist

Forty is a terrible age. It is the age in which we become what we are.
CHARLES PÉGUY, 1873–1914, French writer

Nature gives you the face you have when you are twenty. Life shapes the face you have at thirty. But it is up to you to earn the face you have at fifty.
Attributed to COCO CHANEL, 1883–1971, fashion designer

The man who views the world at fifty the same as he did at twenty has wasted thirty years of his life.
MUHAMMAD ALI, b. 1942, American boxer

The man who is a pessimist before forty-eight knows too much; if he is an optimist after it, he knows too little.
MARK TWAIN, 1835–1910, American humorist, Notebook, *December 1902*

A team of economists, who published their results in the journal *Social Science and Medicine*, have shown that people's levels of happiness are definitely a curved shape. It would appear that we are happiest at the start and the end of our lives, making us pretty grumpy and depressed in the middle years between forty and fifty. This was a pattern that appeared not only in Europe and America, but in countries across the globe in Asia and Africa.

MIDDLE EAST

Iraq probably has no weapons of mass destruction in the commonly understood sense of the term—namely a credible device capable of being delivered against a strategic city target.
ROBIN COOKE, 1946–2005, speech delivered in British House of Commons in 2003

No young American in uniform should ever be held hostage to America's dependence on oil from the Middle East.

JOHN KERRY, b. 1943, American politician, 2004 Speech

It is reckoned the Iraq war is costing the United States about **$12 billion a month** with no sign of decrease or a U.S. exit from Iraq. Providing education for every child in the world, according to estimates by most government agencies, would cost $11 billion a year.

The unresolved **Israel-Palestine conflict** is a festering wound for the world, fueling extremism and strife. A third of people polled by the Pew Research Center, in an opinion poll of 17,000 people in fifteen countries, thought of it as the top threat to the world.

Despite immense wealth from oil revenues, UN sources reveal that Arab States continue to lag behind in terms of education and development. One of the main factors for this, it is believed, is continued discrimination against women in education. **Less than 80 percent** of girls in Arab States, except for four countries, receive a secondary education. Illiteracy rates for girls stand at around 50 percent for some states.

There are about **25 million land mines** still buried in the ground in Iraq. That's about one per Iraqi. They seriously hamper everything from agriculture to prospecting for oil.

Water shortages could soon become the next source of war in the Middle East with drought and human population growth putting immense pressure on dwindling resources.

MUSIC

Music is no different from opium. Music affects the human mind in a way that makes people think of nothing but music and sensual matters . . . Music is a treason to the country, a treason to our youth, and we should cut out all this music and replace it with something instructive.

AYATOLLAH KHOMEINI, 1900–1989, Ramadam speech on July 23, 1979

Music was invented to deceive and delude mankind.

EPHORUS OF CUMAE, 400–330 BC

Music was invented to confirm human loneliness.

Attributed to LAWRENCE DURRELL, 1912–1990

Accordion, n. An instrument in harmony with the sentiments of an assassin.

Piano, n. A parlor utensil for subduing the impenitent visitor. It is operated by depressing the keys of the machine and the spirits of the audience.

AMBROSE BIERCE, 1842–c.1914, The Devil's Dictionary (1911)

I must confess that I live a miserable life . . . I live entirely in my music.

LUDWIG VAN BEETHOVEN, 1770–1827, German composer

You can't mess with people's heads, that's for sure. But that's what music's all about, messing with people's heads.
JIMI HENDRIX, 1942–1970, American musician

So-called "Muzak"—elevator music, canned music, and piped music—is fast becoming a form of pollution. It is part of the background in everything from supermarkets to restaurants and is played to phone-in customers when they are put on hold. The organization to stop Muzak, Pipedown, managed to persuade Gatwick airport to discontinue the use of piped music when the results of a survey revealed that most people were not in favor of it. To find out more about Pipedown's campaigns against wall-to-wall Muzak, visit www.pipedown.info.

Today, what is not worth being spoken is sung.
PIERRE BEAUMARCHAIS, 1732–1799, writer of The Barber of Seville *and* The Marriage of Figaro *in 1775*

Three farts and a raspberry, orchestrated.
Attributed to SIR JOHN BARBIROLLI, on modern music, quoted in M. Kennedy's Barbirolli, Conductor Laureate *(1971)*

At the time of the Third Reich only three composers were really approved of: Richard Wagner, Beethoven, and Anton Bruckner.

The public doesn't want new music: the main thing it demands of a composer is that he be dead.
ARTHUR HONEGGER, 1892–1955, I Am a Composer *(1951)*

NATURE

Nature is usually wrong.
JAMES MCNEILL WHISTLER, 1834–1903, American painter

Nature is ugly, and I prefer the monsters of my fancy to what is positively trivial.
CHARLES BAUDELAIRE, 1821–1867, French poet

The worst human death-toll from a natural disaster ever was the 1931 Yellow River flood in China, with some 7 to 9 million killed.

The principal task of civilization, its actual *raison d'être*, is to defend us against nature.
SIGMUND FREUD, 1856–1939, The Future of an Illusion *(1927)*

Man and nature have such different views about the good of the world.
GEORGE GISSING, 1857–1903, English novelist

In sober truth, nearly all the things which men are hanged or imprisoned for doing to one another, are Nature's every day performances. Killing, the most criminal act recognized by human laws, Nature does once to every being that lives; and in a large proportion of cases, after protracted tortures such as only the greatest monsters whom we read of ever purposely inflicted on their living fellow-creatures . . . Next to taking life (equal to it according to a high authority) is taking the means by which we live; and Nature does this too on the largest scale and with the most callous indifference. A single hurricane destroys the hopes of a season; a flight of locusts, or an inundation, desolates a district; a trifling chemical change in a edible root, starves a million of people . . . Everything, in short, which the worst men commit either against life or property is perpetrated on a larger scale by natural agents.

JOHN STUART MILL, *1806–1873, British philosopher, "Nature"*

Don't know where, don't know when:
Near-Earth Objects are going to hit us

Earth, in the words of one geologist, exists in an asteroid swarm. Astronomers at the Near Earth Asteroid Tracking (NEAT) project based in Hawaii have concluded that there are now about 700 potentially hazardous NEOs (large asteroids or comets) out there. An asteroid is believed to have smashed into our planet 65 million years ago, causing fireballs, shock waves, tsunamis, and then a nuclear-type winter, culminating in the notorious "Cretaceous-Tertiary extinction event" which wiped out the dinosaurs, who had "ruled the Earth" for about

140 million years by then, rather longer than we have yet managed—or are likely to. With a more than 1% chance of an object striking us this century, and causing between 100,000 and tens of million of deaths (depending on where it lands), let's hope it hits later rather than sooner, because at the moment, as Dr. David Jewitt of the University of Hawaii points out, "We have no coherent plan of action should a threat arise."

People thought they could explain and conquer nature— yet the outcome is that they destroyed it and disinherited themselves from it.

VACLAV HAVEL, b. 1936, playwright and last president of Czechoslovakia

OLD AGE

Every man desires to live long; but no man would be old.

JONATHAN SWIFT, 1667–1745, Thoughts on Various Subjects *(1727)*

To speak humanely, death has a useful function: it puts an end to old age.

JEAN DE LA BRUYÈRE, 1645–1696, "Les caractères ou les moeurs de ce siècle," De l'Homme no. 48

You have to live old, even very old, even excessively old. Then you have the pleasure, as years pass by, of burying the people who mocked you.
JEAN DUTOURD, *b. 1920, French writer*

Old age is the most unexpected of things that can happen to a man.
LEON TROTSKY, *1879–1940*, Diary in Exile *(1959)*

In 2000, there were 600 million people aged sixty and over. There will be 1.2 billion by 2025 and 2 billion by 2050. Today, about two thirds of all elderly people are living in the developing world. By 2025, it will be 75 percent. In the developed world, the very old (that is people aged eighty or over) are the most rapidly-growing population group. The mechanisms for dealing with this boom in gray-haired humans have yet to be thought out. In China alone, the elderly population is set to double between 2000 and 2027. The World Health Organization (WHO) is warning that such rapid rises, all around the world, are going to have a massive and disruptive impact on the way we live, from an increase in diseases, dementia and nursing care to the way we run our pension systems, homes and workplaces.

Do I enjoy getting older? No, I'm thrilled and delighted for those people who enjoy the experience. I just don't happen to be one of them.
CHER, b. 1946, May 2004, American singer and actress

Youth is a blunder: Manhood, a struggle; Old Age, a regret.
BENJAMIN DISRAELI, 1804–1881, Coningsby *(1844)*

I prayed to rediscover my childhood and it returned, and I feel that it is as difficult as it was then, and that growing old has had no purpose at all.
RAINER MARIA RILKE, 1875–1926, German poet, Die Aufzeichnungen des Malte Laurids Brigge *(1910)*

Age discrimination or ageism is regularly practiced by employers the world over despite many governments signing up to conventions and laws condemning it.

Thou shouldst not have been old till thou hadst been wise.
WILLIAM SHAKESPEARE, 1564–1616, King Lear *(1605)*

All decrepit is this body,
diseases' nest and frail;
this foul mass is broken up
for life does end in death.
The Dhammapada, *Chapter 11, Verse 148*

ORDER

Chaos often breeds life, when order breeds habit.
HENRY BROOKS ADAMS, 1838–1918, The Education of Henry
Adams *(1907)*

The rich man in his castle,
The poor man at his gate,
God made them, high or lowly,
And ordered their estate.
CECIL FRANCES ALEXANDER, 1818–1895, Irish poet, "All Things
Bright and Beautiful" (1848)

Obsessive Compulsive Disorder can be an extremely
debilitating condition in which sufferers, amongst other
things, yearn for exactness in the way things are ordered
or arranged. World Health Organization lists OCD as
one of the most crippling illnesses for its pernicious
effect on work, life and income. It is, by its very nature,
an illness that forces sufferers to keep silent about their
pain; but professionals can help.

In any country there must be people who have to die.
They are the sacrifices any nation has to make to achieve
law and order.
IDI AMIN, 1920–2003, president of Uganda

Chaos, a rough unordered mass.
OVID, 43 BC–AD 17, Metamorphoses

Life creates order, but order does not create life.
ANTOINE DE SAINT-EXUPÉRY, 1900–1944, French writer and aviator, Lettre à un otage *(1943)*

PARENTHOOD

Children begin by loving their parents; after a time they judge them; rarely, if ever, do they forgive them.
OSCAR WILDE, 1854–1900, The Importance of Being Earnest *(1895)*

How sharper than a serpent's tooth it is
To have a thankless child!
WILLIAM SHAKESPEARE, 1564–1616, King Lear

Literature is mostly about having sex and not much about having children. Life is the other way around.
DAVID LODGE, b. 1935, British author, The British Museum Is Falling Down *(1965)*

He that hath wife and children hath given hostages to fortune; for they are impediments to great enterprises, either of virtue or mischief.
FRANCIS BACON, 1561–1626, English philosopher

If you desire to drain to the dregs the fullest cup of scorn and hatred that a human fellow creature can pour out for you, let a young mother hear you call her baby "it."
JEROME K. JEROME, Idle Thoughts of an Idle Fellow *(1886)*

A mother loves the child more than the father does, for she knows it's her own, while he only thinks it is.
MENANDER, 342–293 BC, Greek playwright

My father was frightened of his mother; I was frightened of my father, and I am damned well going to see to it that my children are frightened of me.
Attributed to KING GEORGE V, 1865–1936

There is no good father, that's the rule. Don't lay the blame on men but on the bond of paternity, which is rotten. To beget children, nothing better; to *have* them, what iniquity!
JEAN-PAUL SARTRE, 1905–1980, "Lire," Les Mots *(1964)*

As fathers go, it is seldom a misfortune to be fatherless; and considering the general run of sons, as seldom a misfortune to be childless.
LORD CHESTERFIELD, Letters to his Son *(1774)*

I have found the best way to give advice to your children is to find out what they want and then advise them to do it.
HARRY S. TRUMAN, 1884–1972, U.S. president

PATRIOTISM

You're not supposed to be so blind with patriotism that you can't face reality. Wrong is wrong, no matter who says it.

MALCOLM X, 1925–1965, civil rights activist

Can anything be stupider than that a man has the right to kill me because he lives on the other side of a river and his ruler has a quarrel with mine, though I have not quarreled with him?

BLAISE PASCAL, 1623–1662, mathematician

I hate the idea of causes, and if I had to choose between betraying my country and betraying my friend, I hope I should have the guts to betray my country.

E. M. FORSTER, 1879–1970, English novelist

"My country, right or wrong" is a thing no patriot would ever think of saying except in a desperate case. It is like saying "My mother, drunk or sober."

G. K. CHESTERTON, 1874–1936, English writer

Patriots always talk of dying for their country and never of killing for their country.

BERTRAND RUSSELL, 1872–1970, British philosopher

Heroism on command, senseless violence, and all the loathsome nonsense that goes by the name of patriotism—how passionately I hate them!

ALBERT EINSTEIN, 1879–1955, German-born physicist

Patriotism is often an arbitrary veneration of real estate above principles.

GEORGE JEAN NATHAN, 1882–1958, American essayist

If I knew something that would serve my country but would harm mankind, I would never reveal it; for I am a citizen of humanity first and by necessity, and a citizen of France second, and only by accident.

MONTESQUIEU, 1689–1755, French philosopher

It is lamentable, that to be a good patriot one must become the enemy of the rest of mankind.

VOLTAIRE, 1694–1778, Philosophical Dictionary (1764)

Patriotism is the last refuge of the sculptor.

WILLIAM PLOMER, 1903–1973, South African-born English writer

POLITICS

You have all the characteristics of a popular politician: a horrible voice, bad breeding, and a vulgar manner.

ARISTOPHANES, 450–388 BC, Greek dramatist

There is no art which one government sooner learns of another than that of draining money from the pockets of other people.

ADAM SMITH, 1723–1790, Scottish economist

In October 2001, a year after his election triumph and a few weeks after the 9/11 attacks, a Gallup poll survey found that President George W. Bush enjoyed 90 percent approval ratings among the American public. In February 2008, just 19 percent of Americans said they approved of the way Bush was handling his job.

Results of poll by Quinnipiac University poll in 2006 which asked U.S. voters who was the worst President since 1945:

George W. Bush (34%)
Richard Nixon (17%)
Bill Clinton (16%)
Jimmy Carter (13%)
Lyndon Johnson (4%)
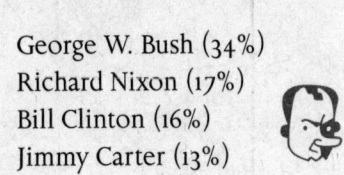

That grand impostor, that loathsome hypocrite, that detestable traitor, that prodigy of nature, that opprobrium of mankind, that landscape of iniquity, that sink of sin, that compendium of baseness who now calls himself our Protector.

THE ANABAPTISTS, in an address to King Charles II, on Oliver Cromwell

I don't go to the House of Lords any more. I did go once but a bishop stole my umbrella.
LORD BERNERS, *1883–1950, British composer*

Democracy will be dead by 1950.
JOHN LANGDON-DAVIES, *1897–1971, British writer,* A Short History of the Future *(1936)*

When a nation's young men are conservative, its funeral bell is already rung.

Henry Ward Beecher, Proverbs from Plymouth Pulpit *(1887)*

One of the penalties for refusing to participate in politics is that you end up being governed by your inferiors.

Plato

Washington, D.C.: Too small to be a state but too large to be an asylum for the mentally deranged.

Anne Burford, 1942–2004, American environmentalist

Men enter local politics solely as a result of being unhappily married.

C. Northcote Parkinson, 1909–1993, Parkinson's Law *(1958)*

RELIGION

Man is the religious animal. He is the only religious animal. He is the only animal that has the True Religion—several of them. He is the only animal that loves his neighbor as himself and cuts his throat, if his theology isn't straight. He has made a graveyard of the globe in trying his honest best to smooth his brother's path to happiness and heaven.

Mark Twain, 1835–1910, American humorist

For most people the Church has become little more than a useful landmark by which to offer directions.
The Archbishop of York

Just in terms of allocation of time resources, religion is not very efficient. There's a lot more I could be doing on a Sunday morning.
Bill Gates, b. 1955, American businessman

The more I study religions the more I am convinced that man never worshipped anything but himself.
Sir Richard Francis Burton, 1821–1890, English explorer and writer

We have just enough religion to make us hate, but not enough to make us love one another.
Jonathan Swift, 1667–1745, Thoughts on Various Subjects

Religion has much blood on its hands, thanks to such wholesale slaughters as the various Crusades of the Middle Ages, estimated at around 100,000 lives; the burning alive of witches, tens of thousands; the Spanish Inquisition (1478–1834), around thirty thousand, and it is, of course, impossible to estimate just how many have died in wars fought in the names of various gods.

Religions are not imaginative, not poetic, not soulful. On the contrary, they are parochial, small-minded, niggardly with the human imagination, precisely where science is generous.
Richard Dawkins, b. 1941, British biologist

To become a popular religion, it is only necessary for a superstition to enslave a philosophy.
WILLIAM RALPH INGE, 1860–1954, Idea of Progress *(1920)*

Religion is comparable to a childhood neurosis.
SIGMUND FREUD, 1856–1939

I simply haven't the nerve to imagine a being, a force, a cause which keeps the planets revolving in their orbits, and then suddenly stops in order to give me a bicycle with three speeds.
QUENTIN CRISP, 1908–1999, English writer

SCIENCE

I am sorry to say that there is too much point to the wisecrack that life is extinct on other planets because their scientists were more advanced than ours.
JOHN F. KENNEDY, 1917–1963, U.S. president, Speech, 1959

For a list of all the ways technology has failed to improve the quality of life, please press three.
ALICE KAHN, b. 1943, American writer

Science is the record of dead religions.
OSCAR WILDE, 1854–1900, Phrases and Philosophies for the Use of the Young *(1894)*

A science is any discipline in which the fool of this generation can go beyond the point reached by the genius of the last generation.

Max Gluckman, 1911–1975, British anthropologist, Politics, Law and Ritual *(1965)*

The only thing that science has done for man in the last hundred years is to create for him fresh moral problems.

Lord Fisher, 1887–1972, Archbishop of Canterbury, The Observer, *1950*

The road to Hell is paved with good inventions.

F. L. Lucas, 1894–1967, English critic

About the Telephone

This "telephone" has too many shortcomings to be seriously considered as a means of communication. This device is inherently of no value to us.

Western Union Internal Memo

About the Gramophone

Sirs, I have tested your machine. It adds a new terror to life and makes death a long-felt want.

Herbert Beerbohm-Tree, 1853–1917, English actor-manager

About the Railways

I fear that the development of railways will destroy the need for waterproof coats.

Attributed to CHARLES MACKINTOSH, 1766–1843, inventor of the Mackintosh raincoat

About Printing

The greatest misfortune that ever befell man was the invention of printing. Printing has destroyed education . . .

BENJAMIN DISRAELI, 1804–1881, British statesman

About Computers

There is no reason anyone would want a computer in their home.

KEN OLSON, president of Digital Equipment Corp, 1977

I think there is a world market for maybe five computers.

THOMAS J. WATSON, 1874–1956, president of IBM

To err is human, but to really foul things up requires a computer.

Farmers Almanac, *1978*

It is claimed by the International Peace Institute, Stockholm, that almost half the world's scientists—some half a million people—are working on weapons research and production.

If only I had known. I should have become a watchmaker.

ALBERT EINSTEIN, of his making the atom bomb possible, 1945

On the explosion of the first atomic bomb, the "Trinity" test, near Alamogordo, New Mexico, July 16, 1945:

"I remembered the line from the Hindu scripture, the Bhagavad Gita . . . 'I am become Death, the Destroyer of Worlds.'"
J. ROBERT OPPENHEIMER, *1904–1967, American physicist*

SEX

I've tried several varieties of sex. The conventional position makes me claustrophobic and the others give me a stiff neck or lockjaw.
TALLULAH BANKHEAD, *1902–1968, American actress*

People who have died during sex include Felix Faure, President of France, in 1899, while being fellated; Nelson Rockefeller, U.S. vice president (allegedly); Attila the Hun, on his wedding night, thanks to a burst artery; Errol Flynn, the hell-raising film star (rumored); and several medieval popes. Given that relatives tend to conceal the truth in order to leave the corpse's reputation and dignity intact, the true extent of sex-related deaths will probably never be known (although it's estimated that around seven hundred men and women die each year in the U.S. from auto-asphyxiation).

I abhor the slimie kisse,
Which to me most loathsome is.
Those lips please me which are plac't
Close, but not too strictly lac't;
Yielding I would have them yet
Not a wimbling tongue admit . . .
ROBERT HERRICK, *1591–1674, English poet, "Kisses Loathsome"*

Sex

. . . is nothing but the exchange of two fantasies and the contact of two skins.
SEBASTIEN-ROCH NICOLAS CHAMFORT, *1741–1794, French writer,* Maximes et Pensées *(1805)*

. . . is interesting, but it's not totally important. I mean it's not even as important (physically) as excretion. A man can go seventy years without a piece of ass, but he can die in a week without a bowel movement.
CHARLES BUKOWSKI, *1920–1994, American writer,* Notes of a Dirty Old Man *(1969)*

. . . the thing that takes up the least amount of time and causes the most amount of trouble.
JOHN BARRYMORE, *1882–1942, actor*

The pleasure is momentary, the position ridiculous, and the expense damnable.
LORD CHESTERFIELD, *1694–1773,* Letters to his Son

Who is the Greek chap Clitoris they're talking about?
Attributed to LORD ALBEMARLE

Cybersex Abuse

Dr. Alvin Cooper, of the San Jose Marital and Sexuality Center, calls the internet "the crack cocaine of sexual compulsivity." In 2007, he and his colleagues studied 9,000 internet users and found that 15% were "addicted" to sexual sites, spending an average of 11 hours a week online for sexual purposes, with three-quarters of them keeping their compulsion secret.

> (The universal) disobedience of this member which thrusts itself forward so inopportunely when we do not want it to, and which so inopportunely lets us down when we most need it.
> MICHEL EYQUEM DE MONTAIGNE, *1533–1592, French writer*

> I'd rather have a cup of tea.
> BOY GEORGE, *b. 1961, pop-star*

SLEEP

> I sleep like a baby too—every two hours I wake up screaming.
> COLIN POWELL, *b. 1937, on hearing that president George W. Bush slept like a baby,* New Yorker *(2003)*

The average person spends **a third** of their life asleep.

Sleep Tight! Don't let the bed bugs bite! If you're particularly itchy at night you may well have an infestation of bed bugs. Look for the tell-tale little stains on your sheets. These can range in color from reddish to brown depending on whether the bed bugs are excreting while feeding on your blood. Bed bugs cluster round buttons in mattresses, folds in sheets and objects near the bed, or the actual bed frame. There are a number of bed bug insecticides to deal with the problem.

Sleep deprivation is extremely harmful to the body. Experiments show that rodents exposed to continued wakefulness die after a few weeks. In humans, sleep deprivation can bring on disruption of concentration, loss of libido and memory, lower immunity, depression and anxiety. There are no firm statistics on the subject, but it is thought that accidents from sleepy drivers cause thousands of accidents a year.

The sleep industry in America alone is reckoned to be worth about **$20 billion.** Much of this is spent on sleeping pills. According to the UK Sleep Council, which represents the bed-and-mattress industry, two thirds of people say they get less sleep now than they did a few years ago.

There are up to **eighty distinct sleeping disorders**. These are made up of four main types: 1) Dyssomnias, 2) Parasomnias, 3) Medical or psychiatric sleep disorders and 4) sleep problems related to other issues such as pregnancy. **Insomnia** affects 5 percent of the population at any time, and 10 percent will experience it at some point in their lives.

> Living is an illness to which sleep provides relief every 16 hours.
>
> SEBASTIEN-ROCH NICOLAS DE CHAMFORT, *1741–1794, French writer,* Maximes et Pensées *(1795)*

A 2003 study performed at the **University of Pennsylvania School of Medicine** proved that cognitive performance declines with fewer than eight hours of sleep. A **University of California, San Diego** psychiatry study found, though, that people who live the longest sleep for just six to seven hours each night.

> If life and existence were an enjoyable state, then everyone would reluctantly approach the unconscious state of sleep and would gladly rise from it again. But the very opposite is the case, for everyone very willingly goes to sleep and unwillingly gets up again.
>
> ARTHUR SCHOPENHAUER, *1788–1860, German philosopher*

Researchers at **Oxford University** have discovered that the traditional cure for sleeplessness, counting sheep, believed to date from the nineteenth century, does not work because it is simply too boring to keep the mind off problems and concerns.

SMOKING

> When we look down the road, I would say ten, fifteen, twenty years from now, in a gradual fashion, smoking will probably be outlawed in the United States.
>
> TOM CONSTANTINE, *chief of the U.S. Drug Enforcement Agency, ABC interview*

> Smoke your pipe and be silent; there's only wind and smoke in the world.
>
> *Irish proverb*

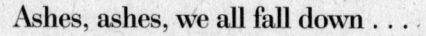

Ashes, ashes, we all fall down . . .

- Smoking and other forms of tobacco use are the second biggest cause of death in the world, claiming 5 million lives a year—roughly one in ten adults.

- There are an estimated 1.3 billion smokers worldwide and half of them are expected to die prematurely of a tobacco-related disease.

- Every cigarette consumed by long-term smokers cuts at least five minutes of life on average—roughly the time taken to smoke it.

- Secondhand smoke contains thousands of identified chemicals, at least 250 of which are known to be carcinogenic or otherwise toxic.

- At least a quarter of all deaths from heart diseases and about three-quarters of the world's chronic bronchitis are related to smoking.

If current smoking patterns persist, there will be about 1 billion deaths from tobacco during the twenty-first century, as against "only" about 0.1 billion (100 million) during the whole of the twentieth century. About half of these deaths will be in middle age (35–69).

Research by Clinical Trial Service Unit & Epidemiological Studies Unit, University of Oxford, published in 2000.

Cigarette smoke contains over four thousand chemical compounds, as gases or tiny particles, including carbon monoxide, arsenic, formaldehyde, cyanide, benzene, toluene, and acrolein.

Synonyms for Cigarettes

Coffin nails
Cancer sticks
Gaspers

Wheezers
Lung dusters

A cigarette is a pipe with a fire at one end and a fool at the other.
Anonymous

TRAVEL

I have recently been all round the world and have formed a very poor opinion of it.
Sir Thomas Beecham, 1879–1961, British conductor

How can you wonder your travels do you no good, when you carry yourself around with you?
Socrates, 469–399 BC

I am wary of globe-trotters: true knowledge is sedentary.
Francois Mitterand, 1916–1996, French president

Car-nage

When Irish scientist Mary Ward was run over by a steam-powered car in 1869, she was only the first in a very long line of victims; today's global death toll on the roads is astonishingly high, with *ten million* people estimated to have been run over since 2000—one every six seconds.

Railroad, n. The chief of many mechanical devices enabling us to get away from where we are to where we are no better off. For this purpose the railroad is held in highest favor by the optimist, for it permits him to make the transit with great expedition.

AMBROSE BIERCE, 1842–c.1914, The Devil's Dictionary *(1911)*

Sir, Saturday morning, although recurring at regular and well-foreseen intervals, always seems to take this railway by surprise.

W. S. GILBERT, 1836–1911, English dramatist, letter to the stationmaster at Baker Street, on the Metropolitan line

The only way of catching a train I ever discovered is to miss the train before.

G. K. CHESTERTON, 1874–1936, English writer

Airplanes have a particularly bad impact on the environment, yielding a warming effect 2.7 times worse than CO_2 alone; and Britons are the worst offenders in the world when it comes to flying, averaging 1.6 tons of CO_2 per person, which is more than double the rate for the average American. Attempts to "offset" carbon emissions are more akin to buying a papal indulgence in the Middle Ages than getting to grips with the problem, and our addiction to cheap flights is only increasing; by 2020, UK airports are predicted to be handling around 400 million passengers, a threefold increase on today's levels. It doesn't look as though people are going to change their holiday habits anytime soon and, as Tony Blair once said, "You can't expect people not to fly." Go to www.planestupid.com for a reality check.

Airplane travel is nature's way of making you look like your passport photo.
AL GORE, b. 1948, Nobel Peace Prizewinner

Why don't they make the whole plane out of that black box stuff?
STEVEN WRIGHT, b. 1955, American comedian

TRUTH

Facts are stupid things.
RONALD REAGAN, 1911–2004, U.S. president

I never give them hell. I just tell them the truth and they think it is hell.
HARRY S. TRUMAN, 1884–1972, U.S. president

I know not what I may appear to the world, but to myself I seem to have been only like a boy playing on the sea shore, and diverting myself in now and then finding a smoother pebble or a prettier shell than ordinary, whilst the great ocean of truth lay all undiscovered before me.
SIR ISAAC NEWTON, 1642–1727, D. Brewster's Memoirs of Newton *(1855)*

Telling the truth loses you friends; not telling it gains you enemies.
JUAN RUIZ, c. 1290–c. 1350, Libro de Buen Amor *(c. 1330)*

Truth, Sir, is a cow, that will yield such people no more milk, and so they are gone to milk the bull.

SAMUEL JOHNSON, 1709–1784, Of Sceptics (1763)

The public does not always know how to desire the truth.

DENIS DIDEROT, 1713–1784, French philosopher and writer

- A lie told often enough becomes the truth.
- A half-truth is a whole lie.

I don't know anything that mars good literature so completely as too much truth.

MARK TWAIN, 1835–1910, speech at "The Savage Club Dinner"

The man who discovers a new scientific truth has previously had to smash to atoms almost everything he had learnt, and arrives at the new truth with hands blood stained from the slaughter of a thousand platitudes.

JOSÉ ORTEGA Y GASSET, 1883–1955, The Revolt of the Masses (1930)

UNITED STATES

Oh Beautiful for smoggy skies, insecticided grain,
For strip-mined mountain's majesty above the asphalt plain.
America, America, man sheds his waste on thee,
And hides the pines with billboard signs, from sea to oily sea.
GEORGE CARLIN, 1937–2008, American comedian, in his
version of patriotic song "America the Beautiful!"

America . . . a nation of two hundred million used car salesmen with all the money we need to buy guns and no qualms about killing anybody else in the world who tries to make us uncomfortable.

HUNTER S. THOMPSON, *1937–2005, American writer*

The breathless haste with which they [the Americans] work—the distinctive vice of the new world—is already beginning ferociously to infect old Europe and is spreading a spiritual emptiness over the continent.

FRIEDRICH NIETZSCHE, *1844–1900, German philosopher*

Favorable opinions of the United States of America among Europeans slumped between 2000 and 2006: from 83 percent to 56 percent in the United Kingdom; 62 percent to 39 percent in France; 79 percent to 37 percent in Germany; and from 50 percent to 23 percent in Spain.

(Pew Global Attitudes Project poll)

I hereby accuse the North American empire of being the biggest menace to our planet.

HUGO CHAVEZ, *b. 1954, president of Venezuela*

The American Dream has run out of gas. The car has stopped. It no longer supplies the world with its images, its dreams, its fantasies. No more. It's over. It supplies the world with its nightmares now: the Kennedy assassination, Watergate, Vietnam . . .

J. G. BALLARD, *b. 1930, English writer*

Every time Europe looks across the Atlantic to see the American Eagle, it observes only the rear end of an ostrich.

H. G. WELLS, *1866–1946, English writer*

It is a pity that instead of the Pilgrim Fathers landing on Plymouth Rock, Plymouth Rock had not landed on the Pilgrim Fathers.
CHAUNCEY DEPEW, 1834–1928, U.S. senator, 1881, New England Society meeting in New York

Sitting at the table doesn't make you a diner, unless you eat some of what's on that plate. Being here in America doesn't make you an American. Being born here in America doesn't make you an American.
MALCOLM X, 1925–1965, civil rights activist

America is a mistake, a giant mistake.
SIGMUND FREUD, 1856–1939

You have to be sure that the Americans will commit all the stupidities they can think of, plus some that are beyond imagination.
CHARLES DE GAULLE, 1890–1970, Time magazine, December 1967

WAR

In almost every case [where the United States has fought wars] our overwhelming commitment to freedom, democracy and human rights has required us to support those regimes that would deny freedom, democracy and human rights to their own people.
GORE VIDAL, b. 1925, American writer

I know not with what weapons World War III will be fought, but World War IV will be fought with sticks and stones.
ALBERT EINSTEIN, 1879–1955, letter to Harry S. Truman

There is many a boy here today who looks on war as all glory, but boys, it is all hell.
WILLIAM SHERMAN, 1820–1891, in a speech in 1880

To a battle lost, the greatest misery is a battle gained. Not only do you lose those dear friends with whom you have been living, but you are forced to leave the wounded behind you . . . At such moments every feeling is deadened. I am now just beginning to regain my natural spirits, but I never wish for any more fighting.
DUKE OF WELLINGTON to Lady Shelley, in July 1815, three weeks after Waterloo

This is the biggest fool thing we have ever done. The bomb will never go off, and I speak as an expert in explosives.
ADMIRAL WILLIAM LEAHY, 1875–1959, U.S. chief of staff to President Truman, on the atomic bomb in 1945

How horrible, fantastic, incredible, it is that we should be digging trenches and trying on gas-masks here because of a quarrel in a far-away country between people of whom we know nothing!
NEVILLE CHAMBERLAIN, 1869–1940, British prime minister, in 1938

The U.S. has broken the second rule of war. That is, don't go fighting with your land army on the mainland of Asia. Rule One is don't march on Moscow. I developed these two rules myself.

FIELD MARSHAL MONTGOMERY of U.S. policy in Vietnam

It's been calculated that there have been only about 230 years of real peace in the "civilized" world in 3,500 years.

What difference does it make to the dead, the orphans and the homeless, whether the mad destruction is wrought under the name of totalitarianism or the holy name of liberty or democracy?

MAHATMA GANDHI, 1869–1948, Non-Violence in Peace and War

Older men declare war. But it is youth that must fight and die. And it is youth who must inherit the tribulation, the sorrow and the triumphs that are the aftermath of war.

HERBERT HOOVER, 1874–1964, U.S. president

I am young, I am twenty years old; yet I know nothing of life but despair, death, fear, and fatuous superficiality cast over an abyss of sorrow. I see how peoples are set against one another, and in silence, unknowingly, foolishly, obediently, innocently slay one another.

ERICH MARIA REMARQUE, 1898–1970, German writer,
All Quiet on the Western Front *(1929)*

WEALTH

If you want to see what God thinks of money, just look at all the people he gave it to.
Dorothy Parker, 1893–1967

A rich man is nothing but a poor man with money.
W. C. Fields, 1880–1946, American actor

Ten Poorest Countries by GNP per capita

Burundi $90	Guinea-Bissau $160
Ethiopia $110	Eritrea $190
Democratic Republic of Congo $110	Niger $210
Liberia $110	Sierra Leone $210
Malawi $160	Rwanda $210

Source: World Bank 2006

Plutomania, n.: a craving for money; the delusion that one is already wealthy; obsession with money.

There's no money in poetry, but then there's no poetry in money either.
Robert Graves, 1895–1985, English writer

He who dies rich, dies disgraced.
ANDREW CARNEGIE, 1835–1919, Scottish industrialist and philanthropist

It is an unfortunate human failing that a full pocketbook often groans more loudly than an empty stomach.
FRANKLIN D. ROOSEVELT, 1882–1945, U.S. president

In the worst stock market crash in history, which took place between 1930 and 1932, investors lost 86 percent of their money. This followed hard on the heels of the 1929 crash when investors lost 48 percent. The markets didn't recover their full value until 1954.

Of the world's 6 billion people, more than 1.2 billion live on less than $1 a day. Two billion more people are only marginally better off.
WORLD BANK

Ten Famous Bankrupts

Rembrandt (artist)
Barbara Bel Geddes (Miss Ellie in *Dallas*)
Handel (composer)
Ulysses S. Grant (U.S. general)
Abraham Lincoln (U.S. president)
Mark Twain (writer)
Daniel Defoe (writer)
Miguel de Cervantes (writer)
P.T. Barnum (showman)
Buster Keaton (actor)
Walt Disney (film mogul)

Repeated research into the effects of wealth on happiness show that when it lifts people out of poverty into comfort it makes people enormously happy, but from there on up, there is no increase in happiness and often a downturn.

In 1923, at the highest point of German hyperinflation, the exchange rate was one trillion marks to one dollar; a wheelbarrow of money couldn't buy a newspaper and the prices on menus changed by the minute. When a student at Freiburg University ordered a cup of coffee for 5,000 marks at a café, and then a second, he was surprised to be given a bill for 14,000 marks.

WOMEN

Unto the woman He said: "I will greatly multiply thy pain and thy travail; in pain thou shalt bring forth children; and thy desire shall be to thy husband, and he shall rule over thee."
Genesis 3:16

Women used to have time to make mince pies and had to fake orgasms. Now we can manage the orgasms, but we have to fake the mince pies.
ALLISON PEARSON, b. 1960, British writer, I Don't Know How She Does It *(2002)*

How to Keep a Woman in Her Place

Foot binding may have been outlawed in China—not before an estimated billion women had been crippled by it—but **female genital mutilation** has not yet been outlawed. There are at least four types of FGM, which may be inflicted, usually without anesthetic, on infants, girls, or mature women depending on the culture. In almost all cases the clitoris is cut off; in 15 percent of procedures, infibulation (the cutting off of all the external genitalia and the stitching up of the vaginal opening) is practiced. Immediate complications include shock, hemorrhage, infection, and death; long-term include incontinence, sexual dysfunction, difficulties in childbirth, and depression. The World Health Organization estimates that well over 100 million women have undergone FGM, mostly in Africa, Asia, and the Middle East, but also in other places where the practice has been imported. The reasons given for performing it include: because it's more hygienic, more healthy, and more aesthetic; because religion demands it; because it maintains chastity in the female before marriage and fidelity afterwards (by making sex painful); and last and not least, because it increases male sexual pleasure. Every year an additional 2 million girls will be genitally mutilated—that's around 6,000 a day.

Only the male intellect, clouded by sexual impulse, could call the undersized, narrow-shouldered, broad-hipped, and short-legged sex the fair sex.
ARTHUR SCHOPENHAUER, 1788–1860, "On Women" (1851)

Written while in medical school:

The Professor of Gynaecology: He began his course of lectures as follows: "Gentlemen, woman is an animal that micturates once a day, defecates once a week, menstruates once a month, parturates once a year and copulates whenever she has the opportunity."

I thought it a prettily-balanced sentence.

W. Somerset Maugham, 1874–1965, A Writer's Notebook *(1949)*

Proverbially, women

- are the snares of Satan

- have long hair and short brains

Furthermore,

- Never trust a woman, even if she has borne you seven children. (Japanese)

- A woman, a dog, and a walnut tree, the more you beat them the better they be.

- There is no devil so bad as a she-devil.

And biblically,

- As a jewel of gold in a swine's snout, so is a fair woman which is without discretion. (*Proverbs 11:22*)

- All wickedness is but little to the wickedness of a woman. (*Ecclesiasticus 25:19*)

WORK

It is wonderful, when a calculation is made, how little the mind is actually employed in the discharge of any profession.

Samuel Johnson, 1709–1784, English writer, collected in Boswell's Life of Samuel Johnson *(1791)*

Ergophobia is the abnormal and recurring phobia of work. For many people it is a severe ailment that torments weekends and turns Monday morning into a nightmare. The word was first invented by Dr. W. D. Spanton in the *British Medical Journal* in 1905. He recognized, as many others do, that one can feel properly sick and traumatized at the idea of work and the workplace.

The law firm Peninsula conducted a survey of 1,200 employees and found that four out of five people lost their temper at work, most of the time through **frustration** at another colleague's behavior. This is a common trend across offices worldwide. The survey recommended regular breaks and a good lunch to calm people down.

METRO-BOULOT-DODO *(French)*
The daily grind of underground train, work, and sleep.

According to a study in the *Medical Journal of Australia*, top managers and directors are less likely to have cancer than employees lower down in the work hierarchy.

WORK IS FOR PEOPLE WHO
DON'T KNOW HOW TO FISH

WORK IS FOR PEOPLE WHO
DON'T HAVE THE INTERNET

Bumper stickers

Work is a necessary evil to be avoided.
Publius Terentius Afer, Phormio *(I, IV, 9)*

If you persistently eat in front of your computer or in your office, an Arizona University study has discovered, you may have up to four hundred times more bacteria on your desk than on your toilet seat.

Working in an "**open space**" environment is very stressful, a Cornell University study has found. Even low-level noise in open-style offices results in stress.

In a hierarchy every employee tends to rise to his level of incompetence; the cream rises until it sours.
PETER LAURENCE, *1919–1990,* The Peter Principle *(1969, with Raymond Hull)*

YOUTH

One cannot love lumps of flesh, and little infants are nothing more.
SAMUEL JOHNSON, 1709–1784, English writer

The question that is so clearly in many potential parents' minds: "Why should we stunt our ambitions and impoverish our lives in order to be insulted and looked down upon in our old age?"
JOSEPH ALOIS SCHUMPETER, 1883–1950, Capitalism, Socialism, and Democracy *(1942)*

Youth is something very new: twenty years ago no one mentioned it.
COCO CHANEL, 1883–1971, French fashion designer

He that doth get a wench with child and marries her afterwards it is as if a man should shit in his hat and then clap it on his head.
SAMUEL PEPYS, 1633–1703, English diarist

Youth, large, lusty, loving—youth full of grace, force, fascination,
Do you know that Old Age may come after you with equal grace,
force, fascination?
WALT WHITMAN, 1819–1891, American poet, Leaves of Grass.
"Youth, Day, Old Age and Night" (1881)

Street children are a global and escalating phenomenon, particularly in large cities of the developing world. These children who work and live on the street, often abandoned by their families and society, risk disease and rejection and are generally forced to beg or hawk to survive. An estimated 90 percent of street children use solvents and glues to get intoxicated and alleviate their suffering and hunger. Life expectancy for these children is low. UNICEF estimates the number of street children to be over 100 million worldwide.

The youth of the present day are quite monstrous. They have absolutely no respect for dyed hair.
OSCAR WILDE, 1854–1900, Lady Windemere's Fan *(1892)*

BE NICE TO YOUR KIDS.
THEY'LL CHOOSE YOUR NURSING HOME

Bumper Sticker

Children are haughty, disdainful, angry, envious, curious, interested, lazy, fickle, shy, self-indulgent, liars, deceivers . . . they do not wish to suffer evil, but like to do evil.
JEAN DE LA BRUYERE, 1645–1696, French essayist, Les Caracteres ou les moeurs de ce siecle *(1688)*

ABOUT THE AUTHORS

Over the past decade **Niall Edworthy** has made a poor to modest living as a jobbing hack. An ongoing disappointment to his dysfunctional family and both his friends, Niall spends his days in a cold garage in the middle of nowhere typing nonsense into an old computer with the one finger not yet afflicted by repetitive strain injury. His magnum opus, *Life Is a Bowl of Toenail Clippings*, remains unfinished.

After years spent toiling at various unrewarding employments **Petra Cramsie** left London to face the vicissitudes of middle age. She and her dependants live in a godforsaken, wind-tormented spot opposite the Black Mountains. When she is not up to her eyeballs in relentless domestic drudgery, she spends her time contemplating the exact size, shape, and texture of the handbasket in which the world is going to hell.

ABOUT THE AUTHORS

Niall Edworthy is the celebrated author of twenty books, making him a hero to many around the globe. Commentators say it is just a matter of time before he sweeps the board of literary awards, turns down a seat in the House of Lords, and retires from his estate in the Home Counties to a tropical island, a robust, oversexed, eight-figure-millionaire philanthropist.

In her dazzling early career launching exhibitions, publishing magazines, editing books, and writing for television, **Petra Cramsie** added considerably to the gaiety of nations. She now lives in a rural idyll above Herefordshire's Golden Valley, secure in the knowledge that tomorrow will be even better than today. Blessed with children, Petra often reminds those citizens of a brighter future that a day without a smile is like a day without sunshine.